BLACK FOLKS GUIDE TO BUSINESS SUCCESS

George Subira
BA, M.Ed., Ed.S.

Published by

Very Serious Business Enterprises
P.O. Box 356
Newark, New Jersey 07101
(609) 641-0776

First Printing   October, 1985
Second Printing   September, 1986
Third Printing   March, 1988
Fourth Printing   March, 1988
Fifth Printing   July, 1992

© 1986 by George Subira

DEDICATIONS

This book is dedicated to some of the people who constantly inspire me . . .

To Mr. and Mrs. Edward Gardner of Chicago's Soft Sheen Products, Inc.

and

Mr. and Mrs. Nathaniel Bronner Sr. of Atlanta's Bronner Brothers Products

Black American history has yet to record more exemplary business families in our community . . .

To Mr. Donald Walker of Dollars and Sense Magazine, Chicago— thank you for the *Blackbook International Reference Guide* and for putting true meaning into the word "networking."

To The Reverend Johnnie Coleman of Christ Universal Temple for Better Living, Chicago—thank you for being the exemplary religious thinker that you are.

And finally, to Mr. Tony Brown of Tony Brown's Journal, New York City—thank goodness there is someone among us who consistently calls a spade a spade.

Special thanks to Ms. Shirley Warren of TYPING TRENDS for her extremley timely and competent services.

TABLE OF CONTENTS

Factors fostering the job slot mentality of the 1960's and 70's.
The failure of the job slot strategy to address Black Folks'
problems.

Twenty specific reasons why Black business development is im-
perative to Black people's survival and development.

Overview of Black Business
Pre-Civil Rights Era
Civil Rights Era

Black Attitudes Toward Wealth
A discussion of eleven distinctly negative attitudes that most
Blacks hold toward the attainment of wealth.

Black Business Attitudes
A look into the most common factors that motivate Blacks to
go into business and an analysis of the plusses and minuses of
these motivations.

Development of Customer Expectations

The Black Brain Drain
The problem of the continuous flow of Black businesspeople
into White corporate America.

The Corporate Junkie vs. the New Black Entrepreneur
An examination of two Black corporate attitudes and the struggle to maintain one's sense of self-purpose.

Wife-Husband Business Conflicts

Chapter Summary

How Much Does It Cost?
Developing a comprehensive idea of the word "cost" as it applies to business.

Don't Expect a Lot of Genuine Support
How striking out on your own disturbs those close to you.

The Costs: Intellectual - Financial - Physical - Time - Family Social - Emotional - Value.

Eight specific business opportunities are offered with discussion on why, how and how much.

Comments on advertising and promotion, mail order, colorless businesses, self-education and definitions of success.

A listing of magazines, books, organizations, networks and major Black business events compiled to inform Black businesspeople.

Progressive Bookstores (or where you can obtain this book)

Distributor Opportunity and Form

Introduction

Black Folks Guide to Business Success is a continuation of our mission of informing, prodding, inspiring and encouraging our people to go into business for themselves. In our first publication, *Black Folks Guide to Making Big Money In America*, we apparently touched on issues which a large segment of America's Black community felt were deserving of our concentrated attention. In it, we tried to identify some new answers to our people's needs since many of the old answers were obviously not working. I am pleased to report that the idea of new, bigger and better Black business is gaining a steady momentum in our community. However, our people hold on to their traditions very, very hard and the idea of *employing one's self* is still rather unthinkable and incomprehensible to millions of otherwise intelligent, proud and gutsy people. We have quite a way to go, believe me!

I am plunging on, however, more encouraged than discouraged. For years I have listened to people constantly tell me that Black folks cannot read, or will not read. It never seemed to dawn on many of these people that perhaps this appeared to be the situation because so very few really relevant books have ever been offered to our people. How many college-educated Blacks, for example, really believe that the books they were forced to study in school actually led them to improve the quality of their life? We believe that if you put practical information in a Black perspective (and we definitely believe there is a Black perspective) and make it affordable, our people will buy, read and perform. This book is an effort, in fact, to meet the growing thirst for relevant information, networks and resources for the task at hand, which is business development.

i

The success of our work here at Very Serious Business Enterprises is not measured merely by the number of products sold but is determined by our ability to measure our effective impact. Our materials are not produced for entertainment but to help produce action on the part of our readers. We are happy to report that of the thousands of letters and phone calls we have received, better than a hundred persons specifically stated that as a direct result of studying our material, they started a business, purchased property or both. We feel very proud of that accomplishment and we both hope and expect that it will continue.

Statement of Appreciation

I wish to thank all the beautiful men and women who have helped me to get exposure to our people. Books, more perhaps than any other commodity, need *word of mouth* support and indeed many, many mouths helped get our message across. While I have enjoyed significant support from bookstores across the country, it was always quite obvious that our success was due to our individual distributors. It was the number and the commitment of the distributors that made *Black Folks Guide to Making Big Money In America* so accessible to so many people. We believe that. that will be the case also with *Black Folks Guide to Business Success* and future books as well.

I am tempted to single out specific distributors for their special efforts but that would be impossible to do without hurting the feelings of others. I also feel good that my appreciation is not limited to words. Our distributors made money selling our books. These books are the people's books in that anyone can read them, understand them, use them, sell them and profit (in dollars and cents) from them. We encourage each of you to join our network (see form inside).

Overview

It appears that the decade of the 1980's will eventually be noted as that time in Black American history when Blacks finally embraced the idea that *private business development* was the *real* basis of economic development. Prior to the 1960's our concept of economic development centered on mere survival in a very racist America. After the civil rights gains of the 1960's, Black folks gained access to a number of jobs previously reserved for whites. Our economic strategy at that point shifted from mere survival to placement in specific types of jobs. We thought, perhaps a little naively, that there would be, or could be or at least *should* be, a job for everyone who wanted to work. Black leadership figured that by placing individuals in the available and developing job slots, our economic plan would come to completion. There was a growing support system involving Blacks that seemed to encourage this philosophy as a really workable program.

First, Blacks were gaining very significant political positions in local and state governments to the extent that major metropolitan areas were now headed by Black political figures. No longer were Black politicians identified only with dirt-poor rural towns. Los Angeles, Atlanta, Detroit and other cities were fully representative of the good old U.S.A. Nor were Black mayors the only Black urban leaders. Black school superintendants, police directors, finance people and other officials mushroomed right before our eyes. With these positions came not only influence in policies and laws but significant influence over hiring practices. Blacks finally had an in!

The second major development during the 1970's was the very large increase in the post high school educational efforts of both Black youth and adults. In city after city, two year community colleges either opened their doors or expanded. Our people knew very well that a high school diploma was not enough for a "really good job." These local institutions were creative, inexpensive and generally accommodating to urban residents looking forward to their first college experience. Not only did recent high school graduates attend these institutions but thousands of adults in their 30's and 40's and beyond took night and summer courses until they achieved their first college degree. Many became much more employable as a result of this advanced and often specialized training. Other Black folk transferred to formerly predominantly White colleges and universities to join their brothers and sisters who had already been there for two years. By the end of 1979 over one million Blacks were in some type of post high school educational program. All this education was to lead to the development of a horde of hungry but now also qualified Black job candidates who, in theory, would now be given equal access to the nation's working world. Affirmative Action programs, designed to ensure a fair percentage of Blacks in new job openings, had their hey-day in the 1970's.

The third major development helping "job slot" thinking was the increasing Blackenization of the nation's military service. The end of the draft called for a volunteer army. As a result of the end of the Viet Nam war, there was now less of a stigma attached to being Black and serving in the Armed Forces. The Army, in particular, advertised in virtually every Black publication and flooded the television with ads which promised civilian type jobs, free choice of interests, practical experience and a college fund to boot, if you desired it. As a result, Black youth lined up to enter the military. This was a non-sexist effort, mind you, sisters in droves chose to wear the Army green which they felt would eventually lead them to the green they were really interested in.

Somehow, however the job slot strategy did not work. In spite of the political gains, the college degrees and the military experience, too few of our people were gainfully employed. Our cookies were crumbling. Jobs which always seemed to be there when others presented credentials like ours were now, all of a sudden, gone. The few jobs which did exist now interviewed several *dozen* people for the one slot. Any idea you had of confidence or of being somebody special was quickly killed, whether you had a degree or not.

By 1980, the nation received a new president and with him came a new perspective of what people were supposedly "entitled to." This president, though a Californian, was known to be anything but liberal in his thinking. His attitudes towards Blacks were thought to be insensitive and there appeared to be nothing in his early years in office to change this perception.

Actually, the decline of Black progress started before the new president came into office in 1980. Depression level unemployment, a widening gap between the incomes of Whites and Blacks, tremendous increases in the number of female-headed households as well as the increasing numbers of children born into poverty were all in motion before 1980. If you add to this horror list the tremendous increase in drug abuse and how the related crime plays havoc in the Black community, it is easy to see why we are sliding backward. The question people are asking is, what happened? With a new recognized cadre of legitimate political leaders, a highly educated middle class and the many open doors of opportunity, why are we still in this situation?

Obviously, there is no single cause for our condition today. And even if we could list all the causes, we would argue hopelessly over which causes were the most important or should command our highest attention.

Many Black leaders single out the president as the major reason for our retrogression rather than facing up to the fact that the "job slot" strategy for Black development was insufficient in the first place. Certainly our problems will not go away at the end of Reagan's term of office. Unfortunately, we as a people have yet to come up with a better way of uniting ourselves than to identify a common adversary. In that regard Mr. Reagan would appear to fit the mold perfectly.

In the search for new answers to our problems, a number of us have in fact dismissed the "job slot" mentality as the key to our *personal* future. We believe further that the concept is inadequate for the future of *our people* as well. People seem to be coming around to the idea that true freedom has an economic foundation and that economic development is in fact connected to the development of Black privately-owned businesses. If we examine the last twenty years, we notice that Black business seems to be the one thing which has *not* flourished and grown at the *same rate* as our voters, politicians, college students, professionals and even our income.

It appears that a sizable group of Blacks are ready to commit themselves to use their next years for the development of a business, their own business. I am very excited at being in a position to meet and encourage (as well as be encouraged by) these new-style freedom-fighters.

WHY BLACK BUSINESSES ARE ESSENTIAL

In the late 1970's, there was a lot of discussion in the media relating to the state of the nation's traditionally Black colleges. Numerous articles focused on the Black colleges' difficult financial problems which threatened to close some of the institutions. Other stories detailed how some of the colleges were admitting more white and foreign students and thereby were losing their identity as "Black" colleges. A number of whites were actually making a case that the time for "Black colleges" was over, that if Black students were to get a complete, competitive education, they had better made sure they attended an integrated institution.

Black educators defended the legitimacy of Black colleges in several ways. They pointed to the lower cost of these schools as making it possible for many Blacks to attend college who could not have otherwise done so. They pointed to the fact that a higher percentage of graduates from Black colleges completed the full four year program and do better academically in graduate schools. Black educators also pointed to the legacy of Black colleges in producing Black political leaders and of being a foundation for and a repository of Black Cultural Development.

The arguments for and against Black institutions such as Black colleges have persisted since Black folk have asked for an integrated society over thirty years ago. Each side builds their arguments on a mixture of facts, traditions, statistics and emotion, and each, when given the opportunity, can make some pretty convincing points. Some people would have us believe that the idea of a "Black" church is contradictory to the idea of Christian Brotherhood. Black musicians have for years been angered that Black music was stolen by White artists and milked for the lion's share of the industry's profits. Each Black institution has its supporters and its detractors.

In this kind of atmosphere, it is perfectly understandable why some would question the appropriateness of the development of Black businesses. Isn't the very concept one of self-isolation and limitation? Are true Black businesses, businesses located in the ghetto or are they simply businesses owned by Blacks? These questions are asked in sincerity by people who are genuinely confused as to which direction Black folk should move in the future. In a period of Black history where things are clearly going backward for the masses of our people, what strategies should be tried next?

The purpose of this chapter is to put forth a strong case for the development of Black businesses. If I'm good, I mean really good, I may make you a believer and a doer. That is my purpose. I want to make such a strong case for the need for Black business that you will feel absolutely compelled to develop one or be a part of the development of one yourself. That is the bottom line. It is not what I say or what you believe but what we together can produce that is important. And I say, let there be Black Businesses, thousands upon thousands of them.

I'd like to begin by sharing my definition of what a Black business is. A Black business, by my definition, is a business doing legal and profitable transactions and owned by a person who is Black. Now these transactions may or may not take place in the Black community, and they may or may not serve a Black clientele. The products or services sold may or may not have been developed or manufactured by Black people. And finally, the employees of the enterprise may or may not be Black employees. As you can see, I have a very broad interpretation of a Black business. But I have placed the emphasis where I think it belongs — on ownership, responsibility, and who collects the money.

I'm sure that if a foreigner traveled through South Carolina in the 1830's, they may have mistaken plantations for Black businesses. After all, the plantation was our community. We did the work and developed the products. We were the single most dominant part of the plantation system — except we did not *own* the plantation, make the major decisions or collect the money. Perhaps one *lone* White person did that but it was enough to make that business a White business.

Now I want to be clear that I am not advocating minimum participation of Black folk in Black businesses. I would rather see maximum participation in these businesses but I would try not to allow my personal preferences and goals to color the very defintion of what we are discussing.

So, with definitions squared away, let me proceed to the meat of this discussion. Why do we need Black Businesses?

Reason #1   Job Development

Even though I have sounded, up to this point, strongly against the idea of the job slot theory of economic development, I need to elaborate on certain points. I do not believe that Black economic freedom can be obtained by Blacks simply by preparing themselves for the job openings that we assume White America will continually develop. Point number two is that I do not believe that our brightest and most ambitious people do themselves or their communities justice by serving in a job slot when they could just as easily be running their own company. However, there are hundreds of thousands of people, Black and White, who do not have the desire, the drive, or the mentality to be running a business, and yes, these people do need jobs. The Black community has a large supply of people who need, want and deserve jobs. What I am saying then is that one of the first groups that would benefit from large increases in the number of Black businesses would be the worker group, the people looking for jobs. I'd like to share my view of the old strategy of job development for Blacks by using an analogy.

There is a story often told by Southerners and farmers that youngsters in the cities today believe that tomatoes and stringbeans grow in cans that are kept in the supermarket. The Southerners and farmers feel that one of the unfortunate consequences of urbanization, modernization and mechanization is that young people have lost contact with something as important as the natural relationship between land and food production.

I think the same thing can be said of many Black leaders, who, having seen so many jobs grow out of government services for the last twenty years, have lost sight of the fact that most jobs really have their origin in private businesses.

Where Do Jobs Come From?

It has always bothered me that both the rhetoric and the strategies of many Black leaders and organizations do not reflect the fact that they really know where jobs come from. Jobs — most of them anyway —

come from *businesses*. Businesses develop a job for one basic reason: they have determined that if a person could do that job then that business would make more money . . . period! Businesses do not hire people *just because people are unemployed*; otherwise, they would hire all unemployed people and in so doing destroy the business. Businesses do not hire people *just because they have graduated college*, because there may be absolutely no connection between that college graduate's interests and abilities and what the business actually needs from their employee. Businesses hire a person because that person's job leads the company to make more money.

Among the major corporations, the total number of jobs is being reduced by forces such as automation (the use of computers and robots) and the moving of U.S. corporations to overseas manufacturing points, giving more jobs to low salaried foreign workers. The huge purchase by *Americans* of foreign products lessens the need of America to even produce certain types of goods, such as motorcycles, cameras, stereos, etc. Finally, there is the elimination of jobs by gigantic corporations buying up large and small corporations and combining departments.

Now, all this means that the Fortune 500 Corporations, the largest U.S. companies, are the *last* place to look to for increasing jobs because they are the very ones who are bringing in the large computers, buying the robots and moving the factories overseas. Yet our so-called "leaders" are going to these very corporations for new jobs for Blacks! Amazing! Pitiful! Amazingly pitiful.

The fact is, there are over ten million businesses in the U.S. and these mostly small enterprises need people (not robots) to help them operate. These smaller companies are the major reason that hiring is going on in this country.

The question that Black leaders and the Black community has to ask itself is this: since most of the hiring going on in the country is being done by small businesses, and since virtually every Black business is a small business, do Black businesses have as much responsibility to grow and hire people as any other small business? If the answer to that question is no, then the current strategy by Black leaders (putting all the pressure on White companies to hire Blacks) is correct but the "pride" rhetoric we recite (we are just as capable as other people to produce things and work together, etc.) would be a joke. If the answer to the question is *yes*, then the old strategies are indeed out of date and our people need to see some action and results to support the pride rhetoric. It is difficult to win the respect of other people in the world if they see that you don't really believe what you are saying. It is also difficult to respect yourself when you can see that too few of the world's people respect you. Black businesses, like other businesses, should not hire the unemployed simply because they are unemployed. Obviously, the weakest part of the economic sector can't be expected to shoulder a weight that even much stronger companies cannot handle. Black businesses should hire folk because they too have done their homework and have determined that filling a particular position will lead directly to increased production, service or organization which will lead to more income and stability. This is business.

If the current number of Black businesses (270,000) were to double and each hired simply *one* new individual, that would be an increase of over a half million jobs. It is assumed that most of these new positions would go to other Blacks. When a half million Black folk get back on the payrolls, all kinds of other good things begin to happen in the Black community.

Black Labor Obsolescence

What are the options in the Black community if we were to fail to develop Black businesses? Obviously, I do not have a crystal ball nor any other fortune telling equipment. However, I *can* read trends and the trend in the United States is moving very quickly towards the point where it not only no longer has any use for unskilled labor (Black or White) but America no longer needs many of its *skilled* laborers either. This country was built in large part on Black labor; from slavery to share-cropping and sweat shop factory work. Black folks took the jobs that no one else wanted, at pay that nobody else would accept. But in a "disposable" society, you use things once then throw them away and worry about the waste, trash and pollution later, at the time of crisis.

Black labor is no longer needed to help Americans make their money— White Americans that is. It is the responsibility of Black businesspeople to utilize the now abundant Black labor pool and utilize the skills of people who have been cast off by the greater society. If we are not part of the solution then we are part of the problem. America has become what it wanted to be (some say the greatest country on earth) without significant input of native American Indians. There is not too much difference between American Indian history and Black American history. America may have needed us to get where it is today but it is pretty sure they can go the rest of the way on their own, without us. You may have noticed many more homeless people than you did the whole time you were growing up. The homeless are homeless because jails and hospitals no longer keep people unless it is absolutely necessary. You will see more evidence of *obsolete people* in years to come. Blacks will be disproportionately represented. Black business is needed as an important weapon to fight Black labor obsolescence.

Reason #2 Personal Development — Leadership Training — Recognition

I'm sure you've heard the story about the millionaire who, when asked what's it like to be rich, said, "It was more fun getting there than it is now, after I've arrived."

Strange as it may seem, most of us take a great deal more effort to prepare for life than we do in living life. Many of us go through high school and college being very precise in the courses we select, the instructors we choose and the grades we try to maintain. We study career guides, take standardized tests and may even take a course in how to take standardized tests. We then study how to prepare résumés, work to perfect our interview skills, read the dress for success books and finally land the job.

The job becomes, for many, the end goal reached after this eight to ten year educational and preparational odyssey rather than the beginning of life itself.

Shortly after one settles into the job, a routine is developed and life often becomes dull and boring while one's individual skills begin to stagnate. The readiness for movement, action and change is lost. Like the millionaire, many of us could say that it was more fun getting there than it is now, after we've arrived. This situation is played out by hundreds of thousands of people of all races and colors. But because America is less likely to accept Black people on an equal basis, Blacks tend to be more likely to stagnate in the kinds of limited job slots that we are given. Many gifted Blacks have not had a really new thought or vision or undertaken a new challenge in years. They become like the walking dead doing the same mundane things over and over again.

These people need to start a business for personal development. They have ideas, they have ambition, they have goals, they have determination, but a *JOB* is not the place where they can get the opportunity to explore any of what they have to offer the world. The job limits them. They are told every month that *they are not being paid to think.*

Some people need the challenge of running a business to be what they can be. As employees, we go to the workplace and try to fit into the job. Seldom is the job expanded to fit the true capabilities of the person, especially a Black person. *So Black businesses are needed as the instruments to enable people to develop their skills* in communication, design, negotiation, promotion, sales, planning, finance and idea implementation. People develop businesses, but the challenge of business also develops people, in ways that colleges can't even touch. If people make up the most important part of the Black Community and businesses develop the people, isn't that fact enough reason to have more Black businesses?

But this matter goes far beyond personal development. What about leadership and recognition? On what basis do we presently decide which of the brothers and sisters among us are leaders? Do we merely look at their educational credentials, their church, sorority or social club affilations? Do we assume that just because they always come out to the community meetings that therefore they are activists and therefore they are leaders and therefore they know what the hell they are saying or doing? We live in serious times and the idea of Black leadership must eventually be measured not by degrees and social contacts but by having demonstrated that you have built a concrete, viable entity that did not exist before *you made it exist.*

Business training is such an arena. It is not surprising that many successful business people find themselves in important governmental positions at some time in their career. Often it is not because they run for office but because they were selected and appointed by the people who run for office. It is common knowledge among the people who run America that the people who demonstrated the leadership to establish a business can lead many other kinds of struggles and enterprises. One day it will be common knowledge among us.

Finally, there is something to be said about recognition. As a worker in a company, it is a rare occasion when you get an opportunity to feel your heart pounding with excitement over the public recognition given to you for an accomplishment or a job well done. Perhaps a mention in a company newsletter or a pin for five, ten or fifteen years of service is all that you can realistically hope for. Yet thousands of newspapers, magazines and television programs never seem to run out of people to highlight. Think about it for a minute. Thousands of people get national attention every single week (if not every day). While it is true that many are athletes, movie stars, politicians and criminals, not all of them are. No way. Successful businesspeople are projected in all kinds of ways at award dinners, in newspapers, television programs, on college campuses, and so on. Why should your one glorious moment in life be limited to college graduation? Why can't you look forward to something glamorous, prestigious or important this year besides your vacation? If you are really as smart as all your teachers and relatives have said, don't you think you should be building something else as important as your paycheck? There is nothing wrong with accomplishing great things. There *is* something very wrong however with feeling that it isn't worth it. Business success can satisfy the ego needs that most of us forget we even have.

Reason #3   An Understanding of How the World Works

I don't think it would be too much of an exaggeration to say that most institutions in this world that work do so because they are run like a business. There may not be actual dollars changing hands nor is it necessary for there to be a financially motivated goal. But procedurally, things that work are more likely than not approached similarly to the way one would approach a business. There is some kind of product, service or idea to be sold or reinforced into the minds of the people. There is always some kind of cost for getting that product, service or idea across to the intended party, be they customers, students, disciples, etc. And there is also supposed to be some benefit that the "buying" party is to receive as a result of their acceptance or "purchase."

Business is generally a numbers game. A long line of pleased customers, followers, patients or students reveals that you're in business.

You have not only learned how to set up a financial enterprise but you have obviously mastered a part of the challenge of understanding and satisfying human nature. It is most difficult to have a successful business without mastering a part of understanding human nature.

There are other forces that cause change in the world besides money; natural catastrophes, raw power struggles, disease and even the weather are a few. But more often than not, when we understand the economics of a situation — economic needs, economic causes and motivations and economic effects — we seem to come closer to understanding why things are the way they are.

Black people have struggled for power for decades. We sought power through social acceptance, through formal education and through the popular vote. We have come a long way in this struggle. But too often we find ourselves asking, "Why is this happening?" Black people tend to look at events through a *moralistic* perspective. We tend to see everything in terms of the Ten Commandments and how things "ought to be." But power and morality are very different. Their paths cross very often but usually they go their separate ways. For a people trying to improve their position of power in the world (even if it is only power over themselves), it is in their best interest to understand how the other players are playing the game (especially if the others are winning). Therefore, if money and business relationshps define the motives for other people's actions, then we should learn how they view and do business. If understanding business allows us to predict other people's behavior patterns and values and we *have to* interact with those people, then we should learn about business. *And you absolutely cannot really understand business and money relationships from an employee perspective.* You have to have the weight and responsibility of an enterprise and its employees resting on *your* shoulders to understand, truly understand, what it is like.

With the tremendous scale of business and finance going on between the Arab world, the Jewish world, the European and Asian worlds, it is no wonder why so many of us do not understand what is going on in the world and why. Running our own shops will not make us experts in East-West relations. But you will be surprised, maybe even amazed, at how much more you understand what's going on around you after you have been in your own business for a few years.

Reason #4   Turning the Dollar Over in the Black Community

Economic researchers and Joe Blow down at the bar seem to agree on at least one economic fact: the dollar doesn't get much use in the Black community once it does get in there. A Black worker gets paid from a White concern and that worker spends that dollar almost immediately with another White concern. That dollar's only connection with the Black community was that short stay with that lone worker.

No other person in the community gets to use that dollar. It's in and out of the neighborhood in one great sweeping motion. Observers are saying that this pattern must stop. If there is to be economic development in the Black community, then the community must hold on to the dollar, turn it over so that the dollar is used two, three or more times in the spending and income cycles of the community. In short, the community must be a bucket that can hold water, not a bucket where the water runs out as fast as it is poured in. Now, in order for this appealing process of dollar retention to take place, there must be Black businesses in existence for one to patronize. People spend their money. Americans save only about 5% of their income, which means 95% is disbursed very quickly. Black folk save less than 5% of their income and are greater spenders than the general population. Therefore, one can say that, technically speaking, there should be a greater chance of Black businesses surviving than White's if Black consumers spend a higher proportion of their incomes. Unfortunately, this is not the case and economic development will not happen in our areas until we have enough businesses to capture more of the consumer dollars and hold on to them for longer and more useful periods of time.

Reason #5   Getting Better Work Cooperation Among Black People

Black people are overwhelmingly (about 99%) employees and they get paid to do specific functions. Most employees eventually develop what I call an "employee mentality." An employee mentality is a narrow and a limited perspective. It says I am only concerned with what I get paid to do. I will only do what I get paid to do, and I will very often do as little as I can do and still get paid. I have a theory that says that one of the reasons that Black people do not help each other is not just due to the reasons that we have heard all of our lives (i.e., slave mentality, crabs in a barrell, jealousy, self-hate, etc.) but because we are so overwhelmingly locked into being employees. As employees, our very first consideration is keeping our job — job security. Our second most important consideration is job advancement, or promotion or status within the company. Thus, when we are asked by another brother or sister to do something, our attitude is not "How can I use my position to help this person?" but, rather, "Will helping this brother or sister threaten my job?" "Will my supervisor or boss think good of me if he or she knew I went out of my way to help this brother or sister?" "Will helping this brother or sister make them look better in their supervisor's eyes and therefore make them look better than me?" "Is helping this brother or sister really part of my job description, is that what I'm getting paid to do?" "Am I really helping this brother or sister do their job rather than tending to my own?" "Will I get credit if I help them do what they are asking me to do?" or "Can I get hurt physically by trying to do what they are asking me to do?" As you can see, the number of questions that a person can have pass through their mind is almost unlimited. At this rate, it wouldn't take long for our employee here to find what for him or her is a very good reason not to do the favor requested of them. The reasoning will probably somehow relate to job security or advancement.

As jobs become more scarce, this obsession with walking the absolute straight line will increase more and more. As affirmative action programs weaken, the concern with job security will increase. As technology advances, people will do what is necessary to please their boss—so that maybe a new spot can be found for them when it is time to play favorites.

What I'm suggesting here is that Black people very often fail to help each other not out of self-hatred or lack of desire but out of the trap of being an employee with an employee's concerns and mentality. Any businessman, scientist or athlete will tell you that progress, growth and success requires *risk*. Employees do not take "risks," therefore many times there is no progress or success in dealing with them. Now, businessmen relate to each other on rather different terms. Businessmen understand that one of the best things that you can have is a favor owed to you by another businessperson. Favors are almost like money. They often lead directly to money. Businesspeople in the best of circumstances help each other make money by forming chambers of commerce, forming formal or informal lobbying groups, and they exchange and barter goods and services in a kind of no-cash economy. Stock tips, investment opportunities and redevelopment programs are all situations where the rich help the rich get richer.

Perhaps it is more theory than reality, but I believe that the more Black businesses come into existence, the more opportunities that the people who run those businesses will have in sharing information, goods and services that will benefit them all. We have seen in the hair care and cosmetic industry that Black trade organizations and trade shows have done a lot to put that industry in an influential position in our community. I have reason to believe that many other sectors of the Black Business World could do some of the same things.

Reason #6   A Business Can Strengthen "Fast Track" Families

The Black baby boom generation was misled in its upbringing and some of the reason why today's problems are so hard to take is because they do not reflect the ideas that were drummed into our heads as children. For example, many of us were told that if we worked hard, retained our sense of values and morality and did the best we could, that we would be a success in life. Being a success in life implies that one would also be happy. It was also implied that if one were to marry a partner with similar goals, habits and values as our own, then a successful and happy marriage could also be expected.

If all this is so, why is it that some of the most unhappy people I know are the people who did all the "right" things? This idea has been pondered countless times over the last ten years by people of all races and income levels. Let us see how success can destroy a potentially happy family.

An intelligent man and woman graduate college and meet in graduate school. Both are very dedicated to their professional goals, whether it be law, dentistry, medicine, the MBA, accounting, etc. This couple meet in graduate school, get married and graduate to the real world. The first few years are exciting, fast-paced and filled with more money than either has ever seen in their lives. Then, at about four or so years, problems set in. There is an imbalance in the career growth. Somebody has really outpaced the other person. Salary levels, job titles, company perks, etc., which started out on a rather even keel, have now greatly shifted to the side of one of the spouses. However, that same spouse has to bring more work home from the office, travel more and spend time at company social functions not to mention serving on special committees. What started out as an even match is now no longer a comparison; one spouse has clearly become more successful than the other. What does this "success" mean for this "ideal family"?

It means that many arguments (petty at first but strengthening as time goes on) about time spent away from home, loneliness and sexual frustration, etc., begin to develop. It means that one spouse loses concern and interest over the latest accomplishments of the other. Why? Because the successful spouse's goals and vision have expanded so much that they have difficulty really appreciating the accomplishments of the less successful spouse. The less successful spouse no longer cares about the other spouse's accomplishments because each new accomplishment only adds to the distance and time loss between them.

Finally, after a few years, one spouse of the other may actually achieve the promotion or position they have dreamed about ever since they were in college. However, to accept the position, they have to relocate to an area that does not have many Blacks and very little Black cultural development. Does this couple live "happily every after" or does "success" destroy them?

The Black baby boom generation could not have been counseled by their parents too well on how to deal with the situation above because the parents had not encountered the situation themselves. Black men and women did not get corporate promotions and besides, a woman's place was in the home back in those days. Today with all our education, designer clothes and extensive credit, we are still out of position in controlling our lives. And the ironic thing is that the more intelligence, education and ambition we have, the more corporate America believes in dictating the use of our time. Obviously, an entry level secretary can quit work at five every day, whereas a competitive middle-manager person must be available weekends and even on some holidays.

Black business offers an alternative choice. In a family-owned business, there is much more room for cooperation and role-playing than self-defeating competition. Rather than deriving individual status from our specific job titles, a couple shares equally in the status of a successful business. Business income is split the way the owners decide, rather than individual incomes being set by outside influences. Although it takes just as much work to make a family business successful as it does to make corporate progress, there is less travel and family members, sometimes including children, are working together. The goals that are allowed to veer off in strange directions in the corporate environment can usually be maintained and measured in the family owned business.

It has always been stated that husbands and wives should work together for common ends. But the words lose a lot of their meaning and the task becomes hard to implement unless there is a vehicle or medium to work together on. A family run business is such a vehicle and an additional reason for having more Black businesses.

Reason #7   To Stop the Black Brain Drain

The example explained in the previous section was designed to show what can happen to a family that commits itself to climbing the corporate ladder. In the example above, it was the personal and family relationships which suffered as a result of this pursuit. However, the example above is also a vivid portrayal of the problem of the *Black Brain Drain*.

The Black Drain is a situation in the Black community where the best trained, most disciplined, most ambitious and achievement-oriented individuals are using their time, training and energy to help the major American corporations make more money. The White business community is run by some of the most capable people in the White community. The Black business community is not generally run by the most capable people in its community because those people are working for a salary, helping the rich get richer. The White business community has the best of both communities and we have the best of neither.

Why should we get excited about a Black person finishing an Engineering or an MBA program at a top university if that also means that we will never see them again? It's like a woman having babies and giving them up for adoption so that somebody else's family can be happy and fulfilled.

Right now we appear to be the only people in America that do not have access to our brainy and gifted people. We cannot afford to pay them what they are worth and they have been programmed against working for themselves. This has got to change.

We need our best trained people to assign themselves the duty of developing Black business for all the reasons that we are discussing right now.

Reason #8   To Take Advantage of Tax Benefits

Very often I hear Black and poor people say that the reason they lack faith in the idea of economic change, whether it be for themselves personally or for our people generally, is because the tax system favors the rich. This is a common belief and one which can be "proven" if one takes the current tax statistics and portrays them from a certain perspective. But questions about the tax system are very much like the chicken or the egg question. What comes first? Was there first an original chicken that started laying the very first eggs or was there first the original egg which produced the first chicken which then laid other eggs? That type of discussion has been going on for years and it applies to the tax system question as well. What comes first? Are there first just ordinary people who, as a result of studying the tax system and following its guidelines year after year, eventually become rich? Or, do people become rich and, as a reward for doing well, get excused from paying taxes by the federal government? Another question might be: At what point do the rich get excused from their taxes? How do you know when you reach that point? These questions, and their answers, will always be controversial.

The truth is that this tax system favors people who take risks and go into business whether they are rich or not. Some of the same deductions that Fortune 500 corporations take to reduce their taxes are also open to you. There are many poor business people who have more deductions and pay less taxes than quite a number of millionaire athletes whose money comes by way of a salary and whose expenses are paid for by the team they play for. If the system favored the rich, the athlete would pay less in taxes than the poorer business person.

If you buy your own home, the system will favor you. If you provide housing for people without housing (rental property), the system will favor you. If you provide jobs for other people (as an employer) the system will favor you. The more you build and do, the more the system favors you. If, on the other hand, you do not take the risks but would rather work for someone who does, then the system does not favor you (employee) as much. If you rent rather than shoulder the responsiblity of a mortgage and property taxes, then the system will not give you the same breaks. In other words, the less you do or produce, the less the system seems to favor you.

The tax system has been and probably always will be controversial.

I remember that I always found myself and others in a very hypocritical situation during the 1960's. We would attack all the inequities in the system during our sensitivity sessions with Whites, yet we would always resubmit our requests for funds (proposals) back to the same foundations. I didn't know the exact connection between non-taxable philanthropic foundations and great corporate wealth at that time but I had heard the term "write-offs" so often that I knew there had to be some connection. The "unfair tax system" enabled the poverty program to survive as long as it did years ago, especially after government funding was reduced.

I am not arguing that the nation's tax system is totally fair and just. But what I am saying is that there is a pattern to the system and you are allowed to learn the pattern. As a matter of fact, the system's guardians will gladly give you information on how the pattern works and how to pay less money into the system. You have merely to ask for it, study it and then do it!

It seems to me that Black folk have three options that they can follow. They can do nothing and pay a disproportionate share of the taxes that get paid. They can stand on the sidelines and complain and preach about how things "should be." Or, they can get involved in business, give employment to other people and as a business person save on taxes in the ways that have been recommended. If tax savings could just allow Black folk to keep 5% more of their total yearly income, that would put 7-8 billion dollars back in Black hands a little longer and that would have a true impact on our consciousness and on our community.

Reason #9   To Develop and Use the Power of Leverage

It doesn't take long for the ambitious businessperson to learn to appreciate the power of leverage. There are many other words that can be used to communicate this idea of leverage. Concepts like credit, credibility, collateral, equity, assets and influence, all can be related to the idea of leverage. Using leverage is having the ability to use what is stable, concrete and of known value to get something of even greater value. For example, few people can afford to walk into an auto showroom and buy a brand new car. Yet, thousands, even millions, of people are driving around in new cars. How did they do it? By using leverage. They presented the auto dealer with a credit history, a down payment, a list of current bill obligations and their job history. All of these factors were considered and the buyer leveraged all of the good things they had going for them in order to drive out of the dealership with a brand new car. The car is security or collateral for the loan. The actual money that changed hands could have been as low as a thousand dollars, or even less.

Just as this concept can work with individuals with jobs and personal credit histories, it can be used for businesses with business profits and credit histories. In both instances, the result of using leverage is being able to physically possess and use something which you could not have been able to pay for in cash. Leverage is credit but yet it is a broader concept than credit.

One of the most fascinating and important things that a Black businessperson can do is to read story after story of how successful Whites got started in business. After a while you can almost write one of these stories yourself. In these success stories, a very key point that I would always look for would be where they obtained their first financial backing. In few instances did their very first financing involve getting the bank loans that many Blacks assume that they get. Most instances of initial financing consisted of a loan against an insurance policy, a credit union loan, money from life savings or second mortgages against their home. But quite frequently the start-up entrepreneur was able to borrow fifty or seventy-five or a hundred thousand dollars from an uncle or a father-in-law. I used to think, "wow! how lucky it must be for somebody to have an uncle with a hundred thousand dollars laying around just waiting to lend it for little Louie's new business idea." But the "rich" uncle was in fact very seldom rich. The loan that little Louie received was in fact a loan that his uncle was able to obtain because he had a profitable business. This is leverage. In this case, the uncle's business is on the line because there is nothing in Louie's background that would convince a bank to lend *him* a hundred thousand dollars. In other words, Louie did not get a hundred thousand dollars *from* his uncle — he got it *through* his uncle's ability to leverage.

If the Black community is to be a significant economic force, we absolutely must use the concept of leverage. We must use what we have to get access to more. Borrowed money is needed not only to start new businesses but to expand existing businesses in order to serve more people faster and better. Using leverage will allow us to begin *lending money to each other* for business reasons.

How do we as a people develop an ability to leverage our assets? Very simply, one step at a time. We must learn to save because nothing develops personal discipline like saving and nothing impresses lenders more than seeing you have the ability to save. Then we must develop our business into a fully recognizable asset. The more sales, regular customers, inventory, and equity ownership of building, fixtures and tools we have, the more of an asset we possess. The more of an asset we have, the more we will be able to borrow. The more we can borrow, the more we can reinvest back into our business for expansion. The more expansion we have, the greater wealth we will be able to generate.

The greater wealth we have, the more we can leverage to start the process all over again.

Many times, lenders use formulas to determine how much they will lend credit-worthy clients. The old figure used to be two to one. That means that if you wanted to buy something for thirty thousand dollars, a lender would lend you twenty thousand if you could bring ten thousand dollars of your own to the table. Today, there are a stupendous number of ways of looking at a deal by the host of private and public lenders in the market place. In a recent television program on the world's richest man, it was mentioned that he was worth about ten billion dollars. This is a mind-boggling amount of money. But what was even *more* astonishing was that the television announcer's next sentence said that this rich man was capable at any particular time of coming up with thirty billion dollars. You can see then by this example, that one is never too rich to outgrow the need to leverage. If the richest man in the world is doing it, what does that say about what *we* should be doing?

Reason #10   To Solve Concrete Problems in Our Community

In the 1960's there was an extreme emphasis on Black cultural and social consciousness which will probably never be duplicated in our history. I was very fortunate to have experienced this movement. During these times of African names, hairstyles, and historical searches for our roots (not to mention the battles in the streets by the "revolutionaries"), there was a definite anti-business sentiment in the Black community. Business was equated with capitalism and capitalism is what started slavery and the exploitation of people in regular, systematic ways. It is my theory that this hard anti-business attitude which was adopted by the first wave of the Black, college-educated baby boom generation has a lot to do with our lack of business success today. It is, however, very easy and logical to understand, especially since we were looking at the African continent and analyzing what European business and Colonialism and Capitalism were doing to it.

However, on the flip side, Blacks were going berserk as consumers. We may not have wanted to be part of the machinery of American business, but we sure as hell wanted the products these businesses produced. The drive for integration in the South and over the nation was fueled by many emotions and principles. One of the emotions was the pent-up desire of Blacks to get on the other side of the showroom windows to examine everything that was available. Black people more than any time previously were now considered a segment of the market to be advertised to, catered to and served. New technology and spin-off developments from the Space program made even conservative spenders anxious to try newly-developed products.

As an activist in the movement, including my days as a Black Studies instructor, I watched all of this with a sense of puzzlement. Why were we so willing to support American Enterprise with our dollars if American Enterprise was so intent on keeping us out of any decent employment positions? But the phenomenon of Black and Third World Spending was a worldwide development. Everybody was buying the Capitalist's products including those peoples still suffering from various degrees of colonialist oppression. Why? It seemed so self-defeating. Boycotting had worked in Montgomery, Alabama, to bring justice, why couldn't Blacks boycott all over the nation for a more permanent sense of justice? That sense of wonder remained in my mind for several years. It took an act against the interests of American capitalism for me to gain insight into our economic system.

In 1974-75, the oil producing nations of the world decided to greatly increase their asking price for the crude oil they were producing for the rest of the world. As cars lined up for a limited supply of gasoline, the power brokers of the nation were furious that such a thing could be allowed to develop. This particular era was called the era of the *Energy Crisis*. The Energy Crisis issues dominated the minds of America for months, even years, as charges and counter-charges were thrown around by and against the giant oil companies. However, one thing was very clear, the American business establishment was not going to sit quietly and wait for this problem to go away. Some bright people realized that to simply complain about the Oil Crisis would do no good. Instead many people went to work on coming up with a business solution to the Energy Crisis. Most people stood on the sidelines and waited. As the answers to the problems started to develop, some called it *American Ingenuity and resourcefulness*. Others called it opportunism and rip-off. The truth is probably something in between.

There were flue dampers, heat pumps, redesigned fireplaces, the return of the wood stove, the return of coal, gasahol made from corn, fuel injection engines, and a million other gadgets to solve the crisis and make money for the problem-solver (energy saver).

The point of this illustration is that whereas the energy crisis was inconvenient and did cause millions of people to argue and complain, this problem was used as a source of money for people able and willing to tackle it. White America may have negotiated with oil rich nations to come down on their prices, but it did not wait for the very people who caused the problem to somehow be the ones to solve it. While they were negotiating, they were trying a hundred different ways to either solve the problem or find alternative energy sources altogether.

This situation of the oil crisis did a great deal to help me understand many things that I had not understood before.

First, the reason that Blacks and Third World people buy goods and services from the capitalist nations is because a great number of their goods and services are designed to address *problems*. All kinds of problems, both real and imagined, are addressed in the form of a product to be packaged, promoted and sold. People are not really buying things, they are buying solutions to problems and the thing being purchased is just the package that the solution comes in. American business has always operated this way.

If you walk down a crowded downtown street in Los Angeles, New York or Chicago, you'll see maybe three hundred people on your side of the street. Some people are wearing glasses for their eye problems, some hearing aids for their hearing problems, some have a knee brace to deal with a football injury from college. One person will have a pacemaker but no one will know it. All of these things are items that were bought to deal with a real problem. But imagined problems can be even more profitable because more people have them. How many girdles are women wearing for their fat problem, how many hair pieces and wigs are men wearing to cover their bald spots. Both men and women are wearing elevated shoes because being short is perceived as a problem to some in this society.

If it is one thing that Black Americans have and Third World nations have, it is problems. If American products can provide these folks a quick fix solution to their innumerable problems, they will continue to buy whether the products were made specifically with them in mind or not. That is why the buying will continue to go on.

Now, let's look at Black American Business. Are the goods that most of these businesses sell problem solving products or just consumable items? Most would agree it's the latter. Why is this so? It is so because Black people have not been programmed to *directly* address their own problems. The black consciousness period of the 1960's that I referred to earlier was also known as the period of the *Protest Movement*. When Blacks did not like something, their idea of dealing with the situation was to simply protest it. On issues of voting, integration of public facilities, etc., if you didn't like it, you were taught that if you protested long enough and loud and or vigorous enough, White folks would eventually cave in and change the situation. It worked and it was very effective as long as Whites continued to feel guilty and continued to cave in and "fix things."

But the 1980's are a different time altogether. Unfortunately, most Blacks still have an old fashioned way of reacting to a problem. When we see a problem, we react with anger, with frustration, and with sorrow. We stop our momentum. We look to see who we can call out to change the situation, to fix it. Most of the time, when a problem hits Black people, we look to the political and economic power of White America to solve that problem for us. If they do not respond, we complain even louder and angrier. If, as many of us must reason, protesting got us all of our gains up to this point, then we should continue in that mode. It's almost like saying if I get this truck or car going by putting it in first gear, then I'll stay in first gear and not concern myself that there is a second, a third and a fourth gear. How much progress can anything make if its locked into the first gear? Very often, it is not the people themselves who do not want to try new ideas but the "so-called Black leaders" who do not want to attempt things that might jeopardize their funding sources.

I'm proposing a new kind of leader, the Black businessperson. His or her funding source is the general public. It is they who have to be retrained and led to understand that *problems are a source of money.*

As a member of your community for many years prior to being a businessperson, you should know some of its problems inside out. You should know the kids' problems, parents' problems, teenage problems and senior citizens' problems. If, as an observant businessperson, you can come up with a creative way to solve a problem in the community, and you find a way to package that solution and sell it, then you will represent the highest form of Black Business and you will get Black Support *because* they won't be able to get that package at other places. That, my friend, is what will change the nature of business in the Black community. When the business person sees themselves as agents of change as well as collectors of money, then Black business will serve our community like American business serves America. The tenth reason for Black business expansion is so that some of the problems in the Black community can be addressed.

Reason #11   A Deterrent to the Wholesale Take-over of Community Economic Opportunities

From the 1920's through the 60's a steady stream of Blacks migrated from the South and traveled Westward and Northward into today's urban areas. In the beginning, when Blacks came North, they undoubtedly were entering someone else's neighborhood because there weren't enough

Blacks to have carved out their own turf. Of course, the largest cities of New York, Chicago and Philadelphia had a sizeable Black population and eventually every city had its Black section along with its Irish section, Jewish section, etc. Efforts by Blacks to expand out of their ghetto's were often met with intense racial hostility and often outright arson, mob violence and property destruction. Because of these threats in virtually all of America's cities, it's not at all surprising that Black folk would be especially possessive about their turf. Whether they were buying or renting and regardless of condition, Black folk needed to feel that it was some place where they wouldn't be hassled. In many instances prior to the integration of the '60's, a virtual Black shopping area existed in commercial corridors. In most instances, however, we patronized the Jewish, Irish and Italians who owned the stores in "our" neighborhoods. The urban violence of the '60's was specifically directed to the White shopkeepers and its was in some ways a statement by younger Blacks to those businessmen saying in essence, "Get out and let us have control over this area." Many shopkeepers were all too happy to collect their insurance money and open up in the new malls that were developing about that time.

Some Black folks could see their own shops in these sometimes burnt out spaces and indeed it did come to pass in many instances. Government programs, Black mayors, community development programs and other incentives, including free consulting services from some of the nation's business schools, helped many a Black business person get their first act together. However, the neighborhoods were changing and the attractiveness of suburban living, the concept of "The Mall" and highways paved with new franchises made the inner city less and less of an appealing place to shop. High taxes, bank and insurance red-lining and the tremendous increase in drug-related crime broke the back of inner city shopping and the boards began to be nailed onto the abandoned buildings. We began to get used to boarded up or raized buildings. It was no big thing. One day it was open, the next month it was closed up and in another year you just might find every damn thing gone but a bare, empty lot where a building used to be.

By the mid-seventies, the Vietnam War had ended and we began to hear the term "boat people." Overnight, we had to get used to all kinds of new people coming into our state, our city and even our immediate neighborhood. Middle East crises caused another group of people to come to America. South American political upheavals and Mexican poverty and Cuban Floatillas and Haitian refugees all combined to add a definite international flavor to many American cities in the last ten years. What were these people to do for a living?

Many came to this country with dreams of becoming rich and they realized what everyone else had known all along: you don't get wealthy working a job but by being successful in your own business. Where are these businesses to be located? The businesses will be located in areas that are underdeveloped economically. They will be located in areas of low rent and little competition. The business will be located in high risk areas but among people who have been conditioned to paying higher prices for their foods and goods. The businesses will locate in facilities that will not require large amounts of capital to set up, stock and promote. The businesses will be set up in places where, if possible, the owner can reside there, thereby reducing their overhead and living expenses. The types of communities that conveniently meet all the criteria above are Black communities. It is at this point that the controversy begins in the Black community as the reactions vary from warm to icy cold. Some community members feel that America is a free country and that all enterprise should be encouraged. Others feel that their community is being "taken over by foreigners" who have no regard for the people they are serving. The great balance of the community seems to experience a puzzlement as to "How do they do it?" The issue is really as much about physics as it is about economics. The law of physics says that two things cannot occupy the same space at the same time. If the capable members of the Black community had developed functioning businesses they would have occupied a space that simply could not have physically been taken by any other person or group.

The new foreign business in the Black community now occupies spaces that are not likely to be lost or given up any time real soon. Even casual observation shows that most foreign businesses do not fail.

If Black business is to exist at all, it must first occupy and hold onto some space. There is only so much prime business space in easy access to the market via public transportation.

Failure by Black businesspeople to claim and function in parts of our community will lead to the continued historical path of our consumer dollar. It will enter and leave our domain in one easy motion. We cannot be a strong people and not hold our ground.

We must find a way to fit and survive somewhere. If we fail to fit in somewhere there will be wholesale take-over of businesses, franchise opportunities and overall economic development in our community to the extent that we would have to seriously question if there really is a place that is "our community." A strong reason for setting up Black businesses is to prevent the wholesale take-over of the economic opportunities in our own community.

Reason #12   Black Role Models, Black Images and Black Pride

One thing that the last twenty years has demonstrated in the Black community is the concept of *false pride*. False pride, as I see it, is a situation where a person grabs onto something and *pretends* that he or she is proud of it out of a *struggle* to find something to be proud of. It is clearly an act of desperation and the object of pride will be discarded or disclaimed as soon as this desperate individual finds something else to hold on to.

Let me explore an example to make the point. Twenty years ago (1965–69), Black Americans "claimed" to be proud of their color, history, hair, mannerisms and overall culture. To many this pride was real. Today, twenty years later, these Blacks have evolved in various ways but not to the point of directly contradicting that which they were proud of twenty years before. To many others, however, their pride of years ago was false in that today what is held dear and sacred is nearly the very opposite of that which was held dear years before.

Some of the values of older people, do not include the value for dark skin or natural hair or Black History and Culture that was seemingly felt twenty years ago. I ask myself, did Black people have a false pride? Were we so desperate for some sense of worth that we glorified some things that we really didn't feel good about? Are we really more at ease with today's nose jobs, straight hair, white women and effeminate men (witness on hour of "Black" music videos) because everybody is free from the pressure of pretending to be proud of things that we always had reservations and questions about? I used to ask myself these questions all the time until I realized a simple thing. Black people were proud of Motown records twenty years ago and we are proud of them today. We were proud of Ebony magazine and North Carolina Mutual Insurance and Parks Sausage twenty years ago and we love them madly today. In other words, there are some things whose sheer power and strength and impression is so real that you are forced to take note, respect and have pride in it whether you really want to or not. Black business, strong and long-standing Black business, is needed to establish true sources of pride to be there when the many objects of false pride have gone away. This is called "institution building," where something is so significant that it outlasts its founders and the original people who made the thing happen. Black people need sources of pride and strong businesses are an excellent reference point.

Virtually nothing is more important to building up feelings of pride than images. We live in a nation that has thousands of radio stations, thousands of TV stations, thousands of newspapers and magazines, thousands of billboards, books, movies and so on.

Media is everywhere and powerful. If you see an image projected positively and often, you will feel pride. If you see an image very often portrayed negatively, you will feel a sense of regret, embarrassment or shame. The central question is who is responsible for what types of images are projected to the public. We know that radio projects images to kids. Radio is run by advertisers. Television also lives by the advertising dollar and ads make the wheels turn in the thousands of newspapers and magazines. A billboard is just one big ad. More than any other thing, advertisers control the projection of images. And who are the advertisers? They are just companies, corportions and businesses trying to get their message across to the public. Black people will never control how their image is projected to the Black and White public until they begin paying for the advertising and they will not be in a position to pay for advertising until they develop the strong companies necessary to finance strong advertising campaigns.

Role models for young children have been a subject discussed in virtually every black school, P.T.A meeting, church and family in the country. But the issues are all the ones that have been presented here. To be any kind of role model you must be a media figure; otherwise no one would ever know that you even exist. Once a media person develops "star potential," some business enterprise has to continually invest money to keep that person *and its product* in the public eye.

Therefore, a very important reason why there should be more and better Black businesses is to control our image to the public in such a way that it always instills more pride in our people and projects positive role models to our young people.

Reason #13   To Support Black Political Candidates

In virtually every country in the world, there is a direct connection between the economic system and the political system, the finance brokers and the power brokers; the United States is no different. In Black America we have had a strong faith in the value of electing one of our own to represent us in that big White House on the hill. The successful voting rights won in the sixties has enabled many a Black community to elect mayors, as well as state and national officials. These politicians were almost always running from church to church, shaking hands, collecting support, bake sale money, chicken dinner money, and various forms of offering money. We have made great strides as a people in the political arena and no amount of statistical analysis should obscure the numbers of legitimate representatives we have elected over the last fifteen to twenty years. But, we do need to do more, a great deal more.

The next phase of political action in the Black community must come from a stronger financial foundation. The last presidential campaign (1984) was a media event more than at any other time in history and there is no reason to believe it will be less so in the future. Media means money. Successful politicians and national figures get media coverage that no one can afford to pay for but they too had to begin somewhere. Today aspiring politicians have to have access to the kind of money they will actually *buy* an attractive and well-known image. This requires the kind of money that chicken dinners just cannot supply. Television advertising, direct mail campaigns, billboard advertisements and so forth can easily go into the hundreds of thousands of dollars.

The central question for the Black community is how are we going to participate in the game if the entry fees countine to escalate? And if more than one qualified Black desires to throw their hat into the ring, how can our community give adequate backing to every qualified candidate rather than continuing to look only for a Black superman? And in those situations where there are no black candidates running for office, how can we use money to help *buy* the best White representation that is available to us? These questions are not a daily constant concern with many Blacks but they need to be if we are to achieve the next level of political power and influence. It is my thesis that the Black business community needs to be a large part of the next phase of electing Black office holders.

There are many ways that a successful business can help political candidates. Obviously, the direct contribution of money is the first thing that would come to mind. However, a business could also supply the very things that a candidate would spend his or her money to obtain. Things such as office and operation space, secretarial service, telephone service, printing facilities, transportation services are only a few. Naturally, the contributions would have to fit within legal guidelines of what constituted proper political contributions. In terms of personnel, businesses have advertising and marketing divisions and the advice on media utilization, demographics and timing could be of immeasurable value to the aspiring office holder.

All of these contributions by businesses to political candidates obviously have numerous benefits to the businesses themselves. Successful candidates now are in a position to throw contracts, contacts and valuable information to those enterprises reaching for growth and development. It is obviously a good public and community relations strategy to "give back" to the community by helping one of their own get in a position of authority. Without question, the political and economic arenas are like two hands on the same body washing each other.

All of the aid and assistance that has been mentioned with respect to companies helping political candidates presupposes that the Black business is on sound footing and well-staffed. Without businesses and their owners being in such a position, we are only describing what other people have been doing, in a winning way, for years. As we rapidly approach the next century and enjoy the comforts of modern living with its satellite communications, etc., it is strongly hoped that we can get past the cocktail sip-chicken dinner stage of political financing. Individuals will always have their ups and downs — personal, financial and otherwise. But if the Black community can develop strong Black businesses, we may enter the next century ready to back elected officials in ways that will give all of us a little more say in the choices and quality of our lives.

Reason #14   Community Service & Philanthropy

In my adult lifetime, I've been to about a dozen meetings where a discussion on Black economic development has led somebody to make a statement something like the following:

> "Well if all these here rich athletes and singers and Hollywood people would just come together and pool their resources, then the Black community could develop giant corporations and feed its poor."

This idea has been brought up countless times and although there is a ring of logic to the idea, it basically reflects a sense of naiveté on the part of the speaker.

First of all, the productive lifespan of an athlete, singer or entertainer is relatively short and even worse, completely unpredictable. An unexpected broken ankle or injured knee has finished off many an athlete before his time. In the world of music, life is like a roller-coaster; today's hit maker can just as easily be tomorrow's has-been. No one knows these things more than the athletes and entertainers themselves and the people who work for and around them. Thus, in spite of the press, pomp and pagentry, public figures always walk very close to the line of oblivion. They have to make their money when they can for as long as they can and hold on to as much of it as they can (after taxes, agent fees, lawyer fees, etc.), because they know that it is a very long way down to the bottom.

Secondly, even if wealthy Blacks were in a position to donate money to causes, it certainly would not lead to the huge sums that the public thinks it would because there simply are not that many Blacks making great sums of money. The amount of money that they could contribute would not even scratch the surface of what poor Black Americans need. So the scope of what rich money could do is exaggerated.

And, finally, we know from reading countless articles and exposés on charities that so much money is spent in personnel and administration of an organized program that only 10% or less of actual monies get to the people it was intended to reach.

So the idea of rich athletes and other "stars" coming together to form giant corporations and feeding the hungry is a pipe dream and reflects the lack of knowledge of the speaker. Of course, isolated efforts like the "We Are The World" U.S.A. for Africa effort is an isolated example of collective action and here too the effort was largely one of donated services (as a singer for a day) rather than out-of-pocket contributions. The U.S.A. for Africa campaign will be a publicly financed enterprise like everything else.

In spite of all of the above, there is a very familiar, logical and historical ring to the idea of the rich helping the downtrodden. Many of us remember during our community organizing days while working with public programs that the very center of the program was the proposal which was submitted to this foundation or that to get money to help the poor. Foundations are usually non-profit charitable extensions of very wealthy corporations whose duty is to give money away to worthy causes. The Ford, Rockefeller, Carnegie and Mellon Foundations are responsible for millions and millions of dollars being channeled into poor Black hands not only in this country but in the rest of the world as well. For all the negative things that one can say about the robber baron founders of these giant enterprises, one cannot deny that many a day care center, senior citizen center and adult education center came into existence because of the funding from these institutions. What lesson can the Black Business Community gain from these examples?

Clearly, it will be many years before any Black Business will be able to set up a foundation that gives away millions of dollars a year to underprivileged people. But I think that the spirit of community giving is something the Black enterprises need to seriously look at for many reasons. The reasons relate to both self-interest and community concern.

In terms of self-interest, the tax laws are set up to allow a no-cost or break-even financial relationship between community giving and taxes owed. Given the two options, I would think even the backwards business person would see more benefit in giving to the community than to the government. Secondly, the Black community will have a negative image of the straight-laced business person (White or Black) for some time to come for reasons that have been touched on earlier. If businesses can get a reputation for giving to the community, the community will feel better about the "idea of business." When the community is programmed to the idea that businesses are givers as well as profitmakers, perhaps more Blacks will entertain the idea of going into their own businesses.

Thirdly, I think that giving has a public relations-promotional quality which is powerful. If two furniture stores are equal, the one with the greatest reputation for giving should theoretically win more consumer support and thereby make more money. For these self-interest motivations alone, I think it makes sense to give back to your community.

On the other side of the coin, there are humanitarian reasons why Black businesses need to develop more of a philanthropic profile. We as a people have been looking to White America for money for decades and for good reason, they had it and we didn't. However, there is a point when a people ought to take pride in trying to correct their own problems themselves. That time is overdue in our community. We cannot continue to tell the world that we are equal but then add that we need a special grant, special consideration or special pity to get over. Black businesses are symbols of Black self-help; it is only fitting that they should be in the forefront in helping our community help itself. Another reason that it is important for our community to help itself is because the Black community is growing in its class differentiation. That is to say the economic and social distance between the Black "haves" and the Black "have nots" is growing very fast. The 1960's "We're all in this thing together " attitude is now in the 1980's a "you get yours and I'll get and keep mine" attitude. Black people need to see other Black people who have gotten theirs but who still care about the plight of the masses. Black business people would seem to be the prime parties to demonstrate this concern.

What kinds of things can businesses be expected to do? Obviously that answer must be developed within the context of the specific community's needs. We know that urban recreational services are at a very low ebb precisely when more Black children than ever are growing up in poor, female-headed households. We know that although the nation is in the middle of the "information age" and abounds with information and data processing industries, Black kids have a horrible time reading and dealing with numbers. Even potential college students need basic level remedial skills to get through the information they are supposedly ready for. A quality after-school tutorial program would be a great contribution by the business community. In Chicago, Soft Sheen Hair Products has launched a national prevention of Black on Black Crime campaign which has been quite effective.

The bottom line is that if a business in the Black community wants to assist, there are dozens of people who are just waiting to point the way. It is important that keen judgement be used by the business person to select how he or she is going to help the poor help themselves. The poverty program of the 1960's demonstrated that all too often it can be very wasteful to just *give* money away however natural it may sometimes seem. Most foundations have strings attached to their money designed to demonstrate a certain amount of accountability and progress. I suggest the philanthropically thinking Black business person do the same.

Reason #15 To Support Talented People

Believe it or not, the world is full of people with good ideas, talent and "potential." As you read this book, there are literally thousands of Black folk tinkering with paints, clay, computers, leather, jewelry, dress designs, etc. and etc. In most instances, they are just as talented as their White, Asian and Hispanic counterparts. Why is it that few of the Blacks will make it while many of the others will? The answer may lie in one word — *backing*. Talented Black people are encourged to "go to school" to refine their skills as artists or craftspeople. Whites very often bypass school and go right into the marketplace to sell their products. Talented Blacks are considered to be valuable properties in the sense that prestigious employers are expected to compete for their services much like professional athletes who take the free agent market. Though it is certainly progressive that Black talent is being more recognized and compensated in the business world, it would be even more progressive if these talented individuals could spawn their own enterprises in the same way that other people do. Of course, quite often artists are not necessarily business-minded in their thinking. In this situation, a good-paying position is exactly what they want and need. But how many talented Blacks are out here in the world with every skill and attitude necessary to make it on their own but lacking in financial backing? Successful Black Businesses, it seems to me, can do themselves, our community and talented Blacks a great deal of good by setting up separate companies in partnership with these exceptional people. Let me draw a picture of what I'm talking about.

Let's say that Fred is an excellent craftsman of leather goods. He makes pocketbooks, briefcases, belts, vests and footwear. Fred constantly draws "oos and aahs" from his loyal clients because of the quality of his work.

He charges top dollar for his work but many of his adoring fans simply cannot pay his prices. Fred has a studio-workshop which he has had for four years and even though he works long hours his income has remained the same the last two years. Fred has the desire and ability to branch out but a bank would not give him the time of day much less a loan. None of Fred's friends have the assets to finance Fred's dream of a larger operation.

Fred lives in a large midwestern town of half a million people, one of whom is John, a 58-year-old undertaker who has had a successful business for over thirty years. John has good business and banking connections and is rather well off himself.

John has the financial connections; Fred has the talent and the understanding of his market. The chances of these two men meeting in the normal course of events in their lives is very unlikely. Not only are they in very different lines of work, but the more than twenty year age difference would likely cancel any chances that they would be part of the same social circles.

In the broader world of ambitious, mostly White, business people, it is common knowledge that those that have money are always looking to make more. Successful businesspeople are often successful because they are involved in several enterprises at once, usually in various forms of partnerships. In the situation outlined above, John, if he were White, would be actively looking for other enterprises to participate in and Fred would be actively seeking a financial backer for the growth of his operation. It would only be a matter of time before John would find out about Fred, and form a partnership.

It is hard to convince Black folk that in many instances in the broader business world perfect strangers cut a deal because each has what the other is looking for — a way to make more money.

This kind of self-help is now needed more than ever in the Black community. Alternative financing is responsible for the economic underpinning of many of today's businesses because of a supreme contradiction in the American scheme of business. That contradiction is that businesspersons are supposed to be willing to take risks while bankers, who supposedly make the majority of their loans to businesses, do not like to take risks. As long as this contradiction exists, and there is no indication of any change, there will be a need for alternative financing.

Black businesses, at least some of them, ought to serve as alternative lenders where other businesspeople can obtain the funds that they are unable to get from a bank. In return, the Black business should be able to obtain a part of the company or a part of the profits.

If there is to be an increase in the number and strength of Black businesses, we must begin to lend money to each other on a legal, profitable and hopefully collaterized basis. We must understand that banks, White and Black alike, are going to always be conservative in their approach and favor operations which are already showing a product and a profitable bottom line.

Reason #16   To Form Larger Investment Groups

I, like hundreds of thousands of other men and women in America, regularly travel from city to city in order to carry out my business. The two things that virtually all of these hundreds of thousands of people have in common is their reliance on airplanes and hotels. Regardless of how many planes one flies or hotels one visits, it is difficult not to think, at least for a minute, what a lofty task it must be to construct and run either of these types of operations. Businesses like aviation, hotels, computer technology, movies, office buildings, etc., are multimillion dollar enterprises and clearly beyond the pocketbooks of Black individuals.

If Black business is to ever get to the point where it participates in larger scale enterprises, it will only be because people already knowledgeable and successful in business have decided to come together in a joint venture.

There have been countless discussions in the Black community about the need for Blacks to pool their money together for larger enterprises. However, in most instances, the pooling of monies never seems to take place. Let's examine why this might not happen. In the first place, people working a typical nine to five job are not going to have the capital to invest in, say, a hotel.

Secondly, even if working people did have the money to invest in a hotel, a question would immediately arise as to who among them had enough business experience to see the project through to completion without being exploited or ruined.

And thirdly, even if an investment group of working people agreed among themselves that they had someone who they felt qualified to take the project on, could they convince a bond or contractor or insurance company that they had the savvy to complete the project on time and on budget?

It takes experienced business people who have developed relationships with bankers, accountants, lawyers, contractors and politicians to take on large scale projects. It takes business people who understand the legalese, the political favors, the tax consequences, etc., and who are not intimidated by titles and connections to see a major project through. This is how it is even when you are white; when you are Black and asking for a larger than usual slice of the pie, the going can be that much more difficult.

In the Black community, we see things moving very slowly toward this level. Motown Records, for instance, has been in the movie production business for some years doing joint ventures with other companies.

Air Atlanta is a Black-owned airline which was only possible because of the economic capacity of an old Black insurance company, young energetic entreprenuerial spirit and Black political muscle.

The point here is this: Black business, as we are discussing it here, for the most part are significant small businesses employing less than a hundred people with gross incomes of perhaps a million or more dollars a year. These are the kinds of enterprises that energetic individuals can legitimately aspire to. But larger undertakings requiring millions of dollars in equity and millions more in financing are clearly going to come about only when proven professionals, comfortable with their own achievements, decide to join forces with like-minded individuals and go for the big deal. Thus, Black businesses are needed to form the bricks which can be used to build the foundation for greater undertakings.

Reason #17   To Develop International Influence

Black people in the United States comprise about 28 million people. Such a population is equal to politically significant nations all around the world.

The income of this nation of 28 million is about 150 billion + dollars a year. That sum is one of the highest per capita incomes of any nation in the world. It is certainly one of the highest incomes of any nation of the Third World peoples in the History of the World.

In regard to education, it can be documented that hundreds of thousands of Black Americans have a college education and all sorts of specialized training. We have been a part of virtually every major scientific effort that America has participated in, from the discovery of the electric light bulb to Space exploration. An argument can be made that Black Americans, based on their talents, education and exposure, are among the most highly educated people of color in the history the of world.

People have said that Money is Power. People have said that Knowledge is Power.

The fact of the matter is that with all the money and knowledge that Black people in the United States have, we are of almost no significance internationally. What I specifically mean is that we are not in a position to use our money, intelligence and sheer numbers to influence what or how things are to happen in other parts of the world. For instance, there are only about six million Jewish people in America and only about twelve million or so people of Jewish heritage in the whole world. Thus there are more than twice as many Blacks in America alone (and there are more Blacks in Brazil than there are in America) than there are Jewish people in the whole world. Now, after you really digest that thought, ask yourself how much national and international decision-making is done or at least seems to be done with regard for the feelings and interests of Jewish people. Then ask yourself how many decisions are done in the nation and the world where the feelings or interests of Black Americans is taken into account? Look at the island of Cuba. It is small and has a very small population as far as nations go. Yet virtually every day one can find an article somewhere in the paper regarding Cuba or Cuba's ability to influence other nations! The nation of Japan is small, only about the size of a few American states. It has about one hundred and ten million people crowded into this area. Yet this small nation is among the most influential nations on a planet that has over a hundred and fifty other nations. And from what we know of Japan, the only thing we can be sure of it that it is going to be even more influential in the years ahead.

Black people are an international factor only as far as consuming the goods that other countries in the world produce. They buy their share of electronic items from Japan, clothing from Taiwan and other Asian nations. They buy Brazilian and Italian shoes and leather goods as well as German and European automobiles when income permits. But they supply these nations with virtually no goods because they produce and export virtually no goods. We help other nations show a profit in the goods they produce and in that sense we are an international factor or influence. But the only two areas that we seem to have made some type of worldwide impact is in the usual areas of music and athletics and very often we do not reap the major portion of the profits even in those two areas.

Why, you should be asking yourself, is this kind of thing possible? How can a people who have money, education, numbers and even significant positions of political power be so powerless in world affairs? I believe a major reason is because our education and money are not concentrated in the form of business institutions which can at any time direct billions of dollars in any particular direction. A business network can direct the energy of a workforce to assist or retard a process that is either for or against its interests.

Are Black Folk really interested in participating in international decision making? Well, if they were not before, they sure were by 1984. In 1984, the Reverend Jessie Jackson was credited with negotiating with Middle Eastern leaders an agreement to release a Black American soldier who had been held captive by one of the Middle Eastern nations. Black America rejoiced out of proportion to the difficulty or gravity of the situation, simply because it was an international act. Had Reverend Jackson won the release of the soldier from a jail in a small Texas town, it would have hardly made the front page of every newspaper in the nation. Also, in 1984 Black Americans were digging in for the long and hard struggle to change the oppressive nature of South Africa in regard to its treatment of Blacks. The South Africans are leading their own fight and this is as it should be. But it is a shame that Black America cannot use its strengths to add further pressure to the South African government.

The bottom line says that Black America must have some influence in world affairs if it is to assume its share of responsibility to free those parts of the world that have yet to be freed. Black business is important in capturing and directing the strengths of Black Americans toward this end.

Reason #18   To Leave Something for Our Children

Black people have been free since 1865. Although we have suffered an incredible amount of racism and problems, there has been time and opportunity to accumulate assets to pass on to the next generation.

Progress for groups and individuals in America has most often been due to what people have accumulated over time, and the type of legacy they were left to work with. Unfortunately in the Black community, we have been employees — when we weren't farmers. As farmers we left our offspring valuable land. In 1920, 12 million Blacks owned a total of 15 million acres. But as we left the independence of farm life and got more involved in the salary syndrome, all we could leave our children was what be bought with our money. Sometimes that was a house. But too often it was simply old, used consumer goods like clothes, appliances, furniture, a car and miscellaneous items with more emotional value than material value. This kind of legacy doesn't leave children anything with which to build on. Yet, they have to compete with other individuals that have been left businesses, real estate, stocks and bonds, large cash insurance policies and other tangible things with which to progress. The Black child has to start from scratch and get what they can get on their own. If they choose the 9–5 job route, they risk putting their children in the same position they were. That is, their children would have to start from scratch also. When a people choose this way to live their lives, it is very easy to see how five generations could live in an area of the city over, say, a hundred years and still have virtually nothing to give to the youngest children which they could use to build something greater. Let me ask you a question. What did either of your grandparents give you to begin your life as an adult? If each of the four grandparents lived to be sixty and if they started working at twenty, that means that each parent worked maybe forty years of their life. If you combine the working years of each grandparent, you can come up with one hundred and sixty years of work. If your answer to the question was *nothing*, then that means that after one hundred and sixty years of work by one generation they have virtually nothing to give to your generation. This is called working for nothing. The next question is, do you think other people work for nothing? Do you think White people, Asian people and other people work in order that they leave their children nothing?

If you are working a 9–5 job, where the income stops as soon as you die (or certainly by the time your children reach adulthood) and if you were to die next year, *what would you leave your children* that they could use to build a better life for themselves and your grandchildren?

Black Americans have been oversold on the importance of formal education and college degrees. *College prepares you to be an employee.* College professors almost never assume that you are going to be running your own company. They almost always assume you are going to be pushing for a promotion in someone else's company. If Black people are to develop power and an economic base, that base must be tangible and measurable. If it is, our children should be able to take it over and develop it to its next stage. Black people must develop businesses to give their children something to use to develop the community.

Along these same lines, Black businesses are needed to *hire* Black young people. We hear so much about the teenage unemployment rate and how much higher Black teenage unemployment is above White teenage unemployment and how this all ties into crime, drugs, pregnancy, etc., and how the cycle perpetuates itself, etc. But the central question is, who should Black teenagers look to to hire them? Should our teenagers get it in their heads that they should always look to White folks to hire them because Blacks will never own a business big enough to hire anybody but the owner? Should Black youth be made to understand that they are going to always have to go downtown and stand in a long line of three thousand applicants for only five hundred temporary, minimum wage, dead-end jobs? Are we to tell Black youth that they can always count on spending part of their money in time consuming public transportation vehicles because their own neighborhood will never have enough jobs? These questions are not questions that White America has to answer. They are not questions that Black youth have to answer. They are questions that Black men and women between thirty and fifty have to answer because if there is going to be any difference in the way Black youth have been treated in terms of types of employment, it will be because these people made it happen. Right now, the rate of employment for Oriental teenagers is much higher in the Black community than it is for Black teenagers in the Black community. Can you guess why that is?

Reason #19   To Better Enjoy The Retirement Years

One of the saddest things in the world is to analyze the frustration of an unhappy employee from beginning to end. Workers start out being frustrated at not being able to get a job as soon as they would like to. Then many are unhappy with their jobs after they get them and look forward to retiring. Yet when retirement comes, there are some mixed feelings about leaving. After experiencing retirement, many feel it is the end of their usefulness and they just sit around dissatisfied and unhappy and in many instances die rather quickly and prematurely. Everyone reading the paragraph above probably knows at least one person who fits into that category yet the question is, is it all necessary? Just because it happens all the time does not mean it must necessarily happen. Most of us know that people who live the longest and happiest lives are most often busy doing something of value and purpose all of their lives. They remain healthy because they are in a good frame of mind because they do not feel that life is over. But when you have been programmed to believe that *you are what your job is*, it is not difficult for us to see why many feel that life itself ends when the job ends, even if its a job they didn't like. Yet, what are the alternatives? Do we keep seventy year old men delivering mail in hot weather and snow? Do we ask seventy year old women to type fifty words a minute? I don't think so. The answer lies in business.

A business is very much like a child in that after you give birth to it, it is a constant concern and source of pride. If the business is strong, it need not die, at least not in your lifetime. Even if you become too old to run your business, you can sell it with the provision that you be allowed to stay on to help make decisions and give advice and share in its continued growth. The problem with most mom and pop type Black businesses is that too often there is not enough of a business to sell, especially if the real estate connected to the place is being rented rather than owned. When a person buys a business, they are really buying a projected income. If the records show that the previous owner made at least forty thousand dollars the last three years, then the buyer expects to make a like amount excepting certain adjustments. But if that business is weak and shows that the owners barely scraped by, then that business will be hard to sell and only at a rock bottom price.

When a man or woman starts and develops a business and that business is strong and profitable enough to be of interest to that owner's children (or nieces or nephews), then it is a much greater pleasure to "retire" because you know that it is not "the end" but rather a new beginning. Even if you do not "work" in that enterprise at, say, seventy-five, you experience every bit the same joy and/or pain in its development as you would if you did still work there. When you can still feel the rush of joy or the hurt or pain, you know that you are very much alive.

When a business owner retires from his strong profitable business which is being run by someone else, it's like watching your grandchildren play. When an employee retires after forty years and goes home, a part of them is childless.

Reason #20   To Make More Money

The final reason we need Black business is so that the Afro American Community can make more money. It is quite well known and quoted that the Black Community receives about 160 billion dollars a year in income (1984 figures) and that sum places us as one of the richest nations in the world. What is not said is that that sum is only 7.7% of all income in America. Since we as a people constitute 12% of the population, we are only about 60% of where we should be in a fair system of wealth distribution. During the Colonial period in this country, Black slaves were to be counted as 3/5 of a man or about 60% of a man. Over two hundred years later, we are right at that same point in terms of income so not a lot has changed in some ways.

If there is a long lagging unemployment situation in the job market for Blacks and if those jobs that do exist are low paying and/or temporary, and if annual raises only about match the rate of inflation, then it should be fairly clear that pure job development is not the way for our people to catch up to the income level they need and deserve. If 92.3% of the nation's money is being distributed to non-Black people, then we have to come up with a way to tap into the larger pool of money in order that we might get to it. The first thing we have to figure out is what do non-black people do with this money. After some research, we discover something not very surprising — we find that they *spend* the money. They spend about 94% (the other 6% is saved). If this much of the money is being spent, it means that the money is moving around from place to place. The money does not permanently rest anywhere, which means we have constant chances to get some of it for ourselves. If it will not come to us in the form of a guaranteed salary and if we can safely assume that it will not be *given* to us, then we are going to have to come up with another way of getting to this money (short of stealing it, of course). If it is *goods* and *services* that people are willing to exchange for their precious money, then we as a people need to tap into the economy of this country by getting ourselves in a position of offering goods and services, so that we can get some of this moving money. How do we position ourselves to get these goods and services that we are going to exchange for money? We are going to have to buy them (at a discounted price) out of the 7.7% of income that we are getting, or borrow money to pay for them. This is called business and that is what we need to do more of. I mean unless you have a better answer.

I have just laid out at least twenty specific reasons why Black folks not only should go into business but *must* go into their own enterprises. There are additional reasons, of course, but these twenty should be enough to get you thinking about doing something yourself. Black business by all means need not segregate itself from the rest of the country and, indeed, it must not if we intend to get at this other 92.3% that's moving around out here. But as to whether Black businesses should exist, as far as I'm concerned, the issue is beyond debate.

WHY TODAY'S BLACK BUSINESSES ARE THE WAY THEY ARE

The last chapter was provided to give a rather comprehensive view as to the many kinds of issues that could be addressed on personal, family, community, national and international levels if we as a people had many more solid Black Businesses. As previously mentioned, the issue of even the definition or appropriateness of Black Business is unfortunately still an unsettled topic in many quarters of our community. Hopefully, some of you now stand much more convinced of the viability of the idea. However, many readers, perhaps even most readers, never had questions as to whether Black Business was a worthy concept; but have instead serious questions as to the capability of Black Folks to develop and run competitive enterprises. Many of us have seen what Black Business owners have called "their business" and walked away discouraged, thinking about just how far we as business people need to go before a minimum level of acceptance can be achieved. This then is the major issue of this chapter, not whether business is ready for Black Folks but are Black Folks ready for business. I would like to approach this vast and complicated topic by offering my opinion of how and why we are the way we are in business.

I would like to say upfront that there are many successful, well-run and well-thought-of Black businesses in communities all across the country. I have been taken to task by some for not adequately pointing out the positives, the good things, in our business world. But in my way of looking at things, my purpose is improvement and one improves by changing or correcting flaws. In order to correct flaws, one must be constantly studying and looking for the flaws that need to be corrected. After all, if you go to the doctor's office with an infected toe, he or she doesn't help you by telling you what excellent teeth you have and how shiny your hair is or how firm your muscles are. The problem is how to heal the infected toe. Positive thinking without some form of critical analysis is no different to me than ignoring one's problems altogether and if you really want a problem to get worse and cause other problems, just ignore it. All of this is to say that this is a critical chapter, a chapter that points to the negatives but more important than that, a chapter which tries to get at why things are the way they are.

In this chapter, we will look at several areas of interest. First, we will look at a bit of history of Black business in terms of how they operated. Then we will look at the changes in Black business which seemed to coincide with the great Civil Rights Movement. How did this movement impact on Black Business?

Secondly, we will examine the general attitudes our people hold toward money. Do they have a healthy attitude toward money? Is there something in our attitude about money which makes us more or less likely to be successful business people? Next, we are going to look at what motivates those of us that do go into business. What attitudes about business do we have and do those attitudes help us or hurt us? What drives the Black business owner, and what seem to be their goals?

Then, we are going to look to see who is *not* setting up Black Businesses in our community. We are going to see if there is any relationship between the increasing number of Blacks who are majoring in business in college and the number and quality of Black Businesses that we see.

What we are *not* going to do is pull out the same old tired list of reasons for Black Business problems that we've all heard before. We are not going to talk about the failure of the SBA (Small Business Administration) to help minorities, or the failure of banks to lend adequate money to small or new or minority businesses. We are not going to blame any particular presidential administration or any governmental cutbacks. We are not going to talk about the inner city problems of crime, drugs, poor police protection, high taxes, high rents, high insurance rates, high unemployment or high anything else. This writer is not claiming that all of these factors do not have a great deal to do with the problems of unsuccessful businesses in the Black community. However, there are other factors which I believe are perhaps even more crucial to our business development but which never seem to get mentioned because they are obscured by the discussion of the problems above. It may seem unfortunate that we have to deal with so *many* factors in our quest for successful enterprise but that is the way it is.

Finally, I'd like to say what I have always said in previous writings and presentations. The problems that I am going to outline here are generally not unique to Black people. What appears to be unique is the *degree* to which we suffer from these problems. The same can be said for our strengths; there are others who run, jump and play basketball the way we do, but the degree to which we do these activities allows us to dominate those fields, nationally and internationally.

Brief Overview of Black Business Functioning

Pre-Civil Rights Era

The pre-civil rights era, for the purpose of this review, will be the years of this century prior to 1954. It is a well accepted fact that the Supreme Court decision of Brown vs. the Topeka Board of Education on the issue of separate public accommodations (in this case, schools) started the modern civil rights era. From 1954, there were a number of other court decisions which supported the civil rights of Black Americans and upheld our right to having equal access to all that America had to offer.

During the early part of the century and right up to 1954, Black people were either not allowed to enter White business establishments or had to enter under rather humiliating circumstances. That is to say, they had to enter through rear doors, side doors, "for colored" doors, or enter into shall we say less decorative facilities. It was during this time that most Black people lived in the South where these practices were the most prevalent. Black businesses at these times enjoyed what we call a *captive market*, meaning that Black people *had to patronize* them to a certain extent because of their general ban from White businesses.

The spirit of these Black Southern businesses was much like the spirit of the South generally — basically friendly. The business people were local people, well known and respected in the community. In times of need, they extended personal credit; no application or credit check was necessary. The neighborhoods were also a lot safer. Unlocked front doors and no youth gangs, drugs or graffitti made people unhesitant in running out to obtain goods in local establishments. These then were some of the factors which made Blacks support their own businesses in the pre-civil rights era. Many Black Businesses survived, it must be remembered, because a set of circumstances forced this support and not necessarily because the businesses were run in a businesslike manner. On the contrary, during the period of time that Black Businesses were enjoying their greatest support from Black people, many things were not happening and it is important to understand what they were. What was not happening was competitive pricing. Black establishments always had prices that were 5% to 20% higher than their white counterparts for a number of reasons, including racism and low volume buying.

What was not happening also, in many cases, was the development of *business standards*. Black people were not going to school to study business for the most part and there were not the multitude of governmental agencies to help business people. So basically business people flew by the seat of their pants. Some may have had some business advice from relatives or neighbors. But by and large, the businesses were set up to be convenient to the business owner rather than designed with customer convenience or product merchandising in mind.

Another thing that was not happening was the accumulation of business knowledge. Each succeeding decade of business people had very little in the way of written materials to study regarding the essentials of sales, promotion, advertising, etc. Therefore, each new business person started from scratch and probably repeated all the same mistakes that dozens of others had made many times before them.

And lastly, what was not developing was the growth of *customer expectations*. Most Blacks from the North traveling or visiting in the South had to learn to expect or accept whatever they found in Black establishments. One of the terms coined at that time was "greasy spoon" restaurants.

To quickly summarize, then, the pre-civil rights era of Black business is noted by the *existence* of Black business but was not characterized by a movement for the *development* of existing Black business. Naturally, there were many exceptions to this rule but they were exactly that— exceptions. Black people patronized these businesses out of a strong sense of racial loyalty, community spirit and convenience. The people did not patronize them because the businesses were "striving for excellence," that requirement or expectation was not present at the time. But the underlying foundation of it all was that the residential segregation and the off-limits status of white businesses downtown *forced* Blacks to patronize their own.

Civil Rights Era

In the 1954 court decision mentioned earlier, the written court opinion included a phrase which said or suggested that separate facilities for Blacks are "inherently inferior." Even though the ruling specifically addressed the issue of public schooling, the impact of the decision was to reach and apply to every facet of public accommodations in every fabric of American life. The move for integration hit full steam in the Dr. Martin Luther King-led Montgomery Bus Boycott in 1955. The sit-ins, freedom rides, picketing, etc., from 1956 to 1969 was the activity that made for a more integrated America. Now, integration was just not an ideal; it became a philosophy — a mind-set. Many in the Black Community thought that *anything* was better if it was integrated.

The feeling in the Black community became split between the integrationist philosophy and the nationalistic or Black Unity philosophy. Some people wanted it both ways. They wanted Blacks allowed in all the colleges in the land but they wanted the all Black colleges preserved in the South. The Black masses were somewhat confused and their minds were manipulated by the strategies used and by the different people leading the Black Movement.

The integrationist's strategy was to get White America to realize that separate was inferior. That something all Black was not as good as something that was integrated. They hoped that most Whites would eventually accept this idea and open up everything in America to people of all races. The problem was that you couldn't *broadcast* that separate was inferior to all of White America without all of Black America hearing it too and being led to believe the same thing also. So many Blacks were actually led to believe that Black was inferior by the very people leading the Civil Rights Movement. These feelings and ideas had a great impact on Black Business. Logically, or according to the logic of the integration oriented leaders of the Civil Rights Movement, if separate was inherently inferior then therefore Black Businesses must be inferior to White Businesses. The problem here was also rather confusing because due to discrimination and internal problems, Black Business did, in fact, have higher prices, a smaller variety of products to select from and irregular service. This would tend to give credibility to the integrationist idea that separate was inferior. Does it follow? Well, it depends on how you look at it. Some would say that all the inferiority of Black Business could be traced to the racism of American Business when dealing with Black business people, or was due to the general poverty of Black America which was caused by nationwide racism.

Whereas a lot of merit is in this argument, it lays all the blame for poor Black Businesses in the hands of other people and no blame or responsibility is directed to the people who had the responsibility of running the business — Black businesspeople. Any analysis which seeks to take all the blame away from one group to place all of it on another group is to my way of thinking incorrect.

But, I'll now get back to the basic point. The basic point to be made here is that a people cannot be programmed by so-called progressive White Leaders and virtually all local and national Black leaders that integration is a good thing and that separate Black facilities are inherently inferior and at the same time not program people against some of *their most valuable institutions*. This includes Black colleges, hospitals, businesses and in some rare instances even churches. The beliefs in White superiority in America had a way of being fought and yet supported by the tactics and goals of the integrationist civil rights movement. I want to be clear that I am not making a value judgement one way or the other. It was an extremely complex issue that involved not only economic, religious, political and social relations, but there were complex psychological implications also. In any event, I think clearly Black Business took a heavy blow during this period because clearly people were led to believe that the White man's ice was colder.

Not only did the all-black is inferior idea kill confidence in the capabilities of Black business but we must also understand that integration withdrew a fundamental reason of why Black business was able to survive in the first place — integration removed the *captive market* from Black Business. Black folk could now spend their money in places that had more selections and variety, lower prices, more conveniences and higher quality goods.

Also understand that Black folk between 1953 and 1969 became more of a Northern People and more of an Urban People. A lot of the positive qualities of the small country store and its friendly surroundings were gone. Black shoppers felt less of an allegiance to Black stores in their new surroundings. Urban city contexts had a general spirit of alienation — everybody look out for yourself quality — among both Whites and Blacks alike.

The "Black and Proud" era in America from 1966 to about 1972 or '73 did not do much for Black Business because that era did not address economic development (with the exception of the American Muslim Movement under Elijah Muhammed). The Black Pride Movement addressed name changes, clothing and hair styles, African foods, holidays, educational programs, Black History, and a host of things including Black dollbabies. Business development was basically incidental to the cultural emphasis of the period. As a matter of fact, an anti-capitalist and therefore anti-business attitude permeated the Black Power-Black Pride era. Struggling Black business people were ignored by the integrationists and chastised by the Black Power people. They were made to feel very guilty if money was on their minds in the 1960's.

Another thing that hurt Black people's patronizing of many Black Businesses in the 1960's and '70's was the death of "mom and pop" type operations and their replacement by a new array of franchise and chain store operations. Most Black Businesses were Mom and Pop operations, principally hamburger stands, auto repair shops, corner grocery stores, print shops and dry cleaners. These were the very type of businesses that were being replaced by national franchises. National ads on television and in the print media brought people into these new operations and many have never thought of going anyplace else.

This then pretty much brings us up to the present. What I hope you have been able to see up to this point are the *conditions* which made Black Business survive at one time under a certain set of circumstances and how those circumstances have now changed so that those types of Black Businesses can be pretty much counted out of the race for today's business dollar. What we have been looking at up to this point are the outside factors affecting the support or lack of support of Black Business. Court rulings, Movements, competition and the like.

What we'd like to do now is switch our attention to the single most important factor in the success of any business and that is the business owner him- or herself. In looking at the Black businessperson as the single most important factor in their business's success, we have to look at them two ways. First, we have to look at them as general members of the Black community with the strengths and weaknesses of that community. Then, we have to look at them specifically as business people with the particular strengths and weaknesses of Black businesspeople. We will look at Black people's attitudes towards money and wealth first.

Black Attitudes Towards Wealth

It has been my experience that Black people have a definite anti-wealth attitude. This anti-wealth attitude derives from a dozen sources at least and at any one time, several causes can be acting upon an individual to cause that person *not to act* in their own financial best interests. The interesting thing is that like so many ingrained characteristics, most people are completely unaware that they have these anti-wealth attitudes and would in fact deny vigorously that they even have them. This can be compared to an alcoholic denying that he or she has a drinking problem or an overweight person denying they have a health problem.

I would like to outline some of the anti-money, anti-wealth attitudes that Blacks seem to have and, where possible, I would also like to give some indication as to where these attitudes originated.

Attitude #1: Black People are a Poor People

A typical belief among Black people is that the race is not only poorer than the general White community (which is true) but that we are poor period! The latter is *not* true. Black people receive about 7.7% of this nation's income. Although that is only two-thirds of the income we as a people should be receiving if income were to be distributed evenly (Black folk make up about 12% of the nation's population) in this country, it is still in the area of one hundred and sixty billion dollars in 1983 figures. As a separate little nation unto ourselves, we would be among the richest in the world on a per person basis. But that is only a small part of the story. Not only do Black Americans have a lot of money but it is evenly distributed money as compared to other nations. The average family income of families living thousands of miles apart are relatively the same.

In addition we spend less money on the essentials such as food, clothing, gasoline, electric and oil than do other people in other parts of the world. We spend less in absolute dollars and we spend less as a proportion of our income. So, the great sum we as a people have is even greater when one looks at the actual power of the American dollar. Finally, we can hardly be considered poor if we only work thirty-five hours a week for this income. Most people work a nine to five job and get one paid lunch hour every day (where no work is done) thus actual working time for most people is thirty-five hours. If you put all of these considerations together, the amount, distribution and power of the dollars we have along with how little work we have to do to obtain them (as compared to other people in the world) then there is no way we can legitimately claim any sort of poverty.

If you accept the figures and observations above, one might ask at least two questions. The first question might be, "If we are not really poor, why do we claim to be a poor people?" The second question might be, "How does this issue of whether or not we are poor affect us as business-people or potential businesspeople?"

My answer to the first question has two parts. The first part of the answer says that if you do not make as much money as the next guy but you want the things that he has, you are going to have to be a better money manager than the next guy. There have been stories of incredible families achieving the growth and development of their members through pure financial juggling acts but they are the exception. On the whole, we are poor money managers and virtually every marketing study of our buying habits says that we are very "brand name" conscious and spend money more out of proportion to our income than other people. I do not particularly blame the Black masses for this situation; I blame people who have been calling themselves "Black educators and Leaders." If people are not taught step by step how to manage their money, why should they be expected to know? And if it is not Black educators' responsibility to teach the masses, then whose is it? Poor money management and over-consumption of expensive goods is a great part of our "poverty cycle."

The second reason we claim to be poor has to do with our traditional means of obtaining jobs and income, asking (begging) the Whites in charge for employment. There has been a historical tendency for us to have Whites pity us to the extent that they feel a sense of moral obligation to give us a job even if there were not one immediately available. Very, very often, this has worked especially with liberal Whites. The best way to get pity is to come in with hat in hand, looking down at the floor and giving every indication that this "master" carries your fate in his hands. Pressure is what has worked. Blacks have gotten a great deal of whatever they have through various forms of pressure. One of the greatest forms of pressure has been "we have to do something for these poor people" type of pressure. Thus, it has *always* been in the interest of Black people, and especially Black leaders, to claim a certain poverty, whether it was totally accurate or not, in order to jerk the tears and the purse strings of White employers, White foundations and funding sources and White politicians. Not to do so would give the White community a signal that we are doing okay and we can make it the rest of the way on our own. Many people will never believe that posture will be a sound one to take vis a vis the White community so they will cry poverty forever.

The second question, how does this issue relate to us as businesspeople, is a very important question. It is important to dispel this notion of our "so-called poverty" for two basic reasons:

1) To change the psychology of the community—Once the Black community realizes how much it has going for itself, there's a better chance that they will think in terms of constructing and producing something rather than begging and spending.

2) The second reason is that we have hundreds, maybe thousands of people who would not consider opening a business in our community because they think it is too poor to support a business. Meanwhile, people from all over other parts of the world come into our community and set up businesses because they know what we don't know. Namely, given the proper circumstances, our community is a profitable place to do business.

More time could be spent to explain why we are not poor, why we are poor money managers and why it is important to dispel the myth of our poverty. However, for the purpose here I believe the point has been covered adequately.

Attitude #2: Money Is the Root of All Evil, or The Love of Money is the Root of All Evil

The most powerful force which programs us against money is the institution which has the greatest support in our community—The Black Church. Most ministers directly or indirectly use the scripture to show how the activity of pursuing money is an evil enterprise. Many phrases in the Bible give a negative reading on people who have or pursue money. The strongest statement goes something like:

"It will be easier for a camel to pass through the eye of a needle than for a rich man to enter the gates of Heaven."

It is absolutely not my intention to be anti-Christian, anti-religious or to cast dispersions on anyone's religious beliefs. However, the church is an institution in our community composed of men, women, beliefs, interpretations, etc. I would think it is in our best interests to critically look at our institutions to see if any of them, including the church, can be improved to serve its members better and still stay within its principles. What the Black Church essentially has done in its history is to bring contentment to its members. During slavery and the earlier half of this century contentment was important to keep one's sanity and will to live. But today the Black Church is still generally programming us to more or less accept whatever lifestyle we happen to be born into rather than to struggle for *material* improvement.

The irony of this institution is that for all the anti-wealth discouragement it generates, the institution itself is the richest in our communities. In the White community, their most impressive buildings are their office buildings or their hotels or their malls, all places of business. In the Black community, our most impressive buildings, sometimes our only buildings, are our churches. In the church we may not learn an inspiring word on how to *make* money but we are made to feel very guilty if we do not *pay* money to the anti-money institution. It is an interesting twist to the idea of the rich getting richer. In thousands of cases of people dying, there is evidence that what the lawyers and the tax people don't get, the church gets. In the Black communities I have lived in, visited, or heard about, money has not been the root of the evil I have seen. The *absence of money* has been at the root of the pain and misery that I have seen.

It is unrealistic for our people to have a healthy attitude about making money if our community's strongest institution programs us against it. I am told that the Bible and other holy books can be interpreted in other ways so as to make clear that the Almighty intended his offspring to live an abundant life. If that is so, then let's do that, let's teach *these lessons* quickly, often and hard because we have to make up for lost time and confused minds. We are free now; what we say in our churches and holy places is up to us. Let us be for ourselves, rather than against ourselves. Let us change this very damaging idea that money is at the root of all evil.

Attitude #3: Money is Only Possible Through The Exploitation of Other People

Black people, if they are nothing else, are victims. We have been victims of slavery, racism, poverty, poor health, unjust laws and penal systems, etc. It is only natural that the victim adopts a victim's point of view. The victim's point of view says that somebody gets ripped and somebody gets rich; there is no other way. There has been a lot of truth in that analysis. Certainly we have known from history that the American Indians, the Mexicans, the Puerto Ricans, the Africans, etc., were all ripped off. And we know today that in many instances the law of the jungle applies. But the victim has to come out of his or her perspective long enough to see that it need not necessarily be that way. In today's world things are not so black and white. Most things are, in fact, confusing and unclear shades of gray.

For example: If exploitation had to be a part of the general goal of making money, then it would be or should be clear to everyone what was or what was not exploitation.

If I go to a fast food restaurant and pay a dollar and change for a hamburger and get it in two minutes and if it fills me up and I don't even have to get out of my car, am I being exploited or served? The restaurant owner may make $100,000 a year *serving* people like this.

If I am a Rock Star and I charge you ten dollars to see my show, am I exploiting you? If I am exploiting you, why would twenty thousand people line up outside, a week in advance, in the rain to buy a ticket if they felt they were being exploited?

If I am a heart surgeon and I charge you fifty thousand dollars to do a heart transplant that will extend your life by ten years, am I exploiting you? Is your life worth five thousand dollars a year?

We each hold different values as to what is important and unimportant, and rarely are people *forced* to pay a price that they think is unfair.

There are thousands of Black folk out there who have dismissed the idea that they would ever have a lot of money. They know themselves well and they know that they could never lie, make exaggerated claims, cheat people, overcharge or steal enough to ever make it in *their* idea of the world of business. I would like to free you now of your misconception. If you hurry, there is still time for you to make your mark and your money. Black victims of America have to escape the victim's point of view if they are to be economically and spiritually free. You must find something of value, offer it at a fair and competitive price and then sell a lot of them and you will be as close to free as you will ever be.

Attitude #4: You Have Got to Have Money to Make Money

It is clear that the many attitudes that Blacks have about money are not of their own making. Many pet sayings, quotes and pieces of advice that we are fond of repeating come from the majority society. The idea that you have got to have money to make money is a popular saying that, unfortunately, too many of our people take as gospel. This idea is a half-truth, meaning just that; it is true no more than half the time. It only takes two things to make money in America: having the ability to sell and having something to sell.

People who sell seldom own that which they are selling. Thousands of people have become rich selling real estate, cars, insurance, furniture, clothes, etc., and yet had no personal investment other than time and a willingness to learn and work hard. Salespeople usually represent someone who has something to sell and match that person and their product up with someone who wants to buy. He or she gets paid either by the party that is selling or the one that is buying and sometimes both. By doing this successfully and repeatedly, one can indeed make a lot of money because there is basically no limit to the number of people wanting something sold or the number of people wanting to spend their money.

In the Black comunity we have a very unhealthy picture of salespeople and selling. As a matter of fact it is interesting to compare the great differences between how the two races view sales.

White Attitude Toward Sales	Black Attitude Toward Sales
Selling is a great source of income; money is *everywhere*.	You go broke selling; *nobody* has any money.
I don't want any *limit* put on how much money I can make.	I need a *set salary* so I can see where I'm going.
I'm going to *learn* all I can about this product and the market and make a mint.	I don't have the *gift of gab* to make it in sales.
The reason I like this field is because I'm really *independent*. I make most of the decisions as long as I bring in the bottom line.	I can be a good worker, just *tell me what to do* and I'll do it.
You know once you learn how to sell its almost *impossible to be unemployed*; there are always openings in sales.	The people I know in sales *can't be doing that great*; every time you look up, they're selling something different.
This field is great; I deal with people from *all over the world—* the Middle East, Africa, India, Russia, Europe, and the Far East, especially Japan and South Korea.	Hey, you know you can't make any money dealing with White Folks; they *only spend it among themselves.*
I started with that there *desk full of applications* and thirty-five dollars in my pocket. Now I guess you can say I'm *rich*.	Well you know what *they always say*, it takes money to make money.

Obviously, it would be grossly unfair to lead anyone to believe that all White's fit on their side of the column and all Blacks on theirs. There are, in fact, hundreds of thousands, probably millions, of Whites who think exactly like Blacks on the issue of sales. And there are probably a few thousand Blacks who view the opportunities in sales much like the rest of the business community. But the point is true, I think, that Black America does suffer with a strong anti-sales bias and this bias blinds us to the means by which people who did not have money got into a position of having a lot of money.

The other reason that the "you got to have money to make money idea" is a half-truth is due to a concept called *credit*. Credit is what makes the world go around—not money per se. The most important things you will purchase in your life will be on credit. Your house, your car, your furniture—even an extended hospital stay will be based on credit. It is important to understand that businesses are also bought largely on credit. If a business is designed to make money, and if they are bought not for cash but on credit, doesn't this further weaken the idea that you have to have money to make money?

Attitude #5: White Folks Are Not going To Let Black People Make Any Real Money

The attitude that White People will not *let* Black People make big money is revealing in several ways. First of all it reveals a slave mentality in that it grants superior power to Whites and minimizes the power of *determination* among any oppressed people. Secondly it reveals an ignorance of present reality: most of the Blacks today who are millionaires are paid directly *by* Whites for their services as athletes, musicians and entertainers in direct contradiction to the predominant attitude. Thirdly, it reveals an ignorance on the part of the believer as to how most big money is made in the first place.

However, from the perspective of the masses, it *is easy* to see why they think this way. The real danger of a half-truth is that one can give strong proof to whatever half they wish to believe in. Unfortunately few of us ever see the complete picture of any particular thing; we see the side we are most interested in seeing, or the side that somebody wants us to see. But there is almost always another side. Let us look at this attitude of Blacks from both sides in order to get some clarity.

Because of the long history of the Black business and professional group in our community being so small and having so few employees, better than ninety-five percent of our people worked for a White business or person or the government. They worked for a salary which was paid by that White employer. Because of the discrimination in hiring and promoting policies in America, it was always quite correct to assume that White folks were not going to *let* Blacks many any *real* money.

Furthermore, the Black business and professional group, although able to live better than most, were for a very long time limited to serving only their own people who collectively represented only 5–6% of the nation's total income. So the historical, social, political and racial barriers were another means of White folks "preventing" Blacks from making any real money.

In those rare instances when a Black business or professional person became a bonafide financial success, very little was ever mentioned about it. The media, white and black, did not choose to do much in the way of "exclusive stories" and those stories that were done were very superficial in terms of revealing much practical advice.

Black successful people, unlike White ones, are not very often interested in writing and publishing their life story or how-to type documents in order to pass on their hard-won knowledge to the next generation.

If the Black Public cannot get the story of the "exceptional ones" from White Media, Black Media or the successful people themselves, how are they to know that these people even exist much less how they did it. This brings most Black Folk right back to where we began, namely the belief that Whites would not allow Blacks to make big money.

In the 1970's and 80's the great national and international changes have made for remarkable opportunities to blast away forever the idea that Whites won't let Blacks make any big money. If we look at sheer numbers, they are revealing. As of the mid-1980's there are over 700,000 people who are worth a million dollars and the prediction is that before the year 2000 there will be a million millionaires. The yearly growth of the number of millionaires is approaching twenty thousand a year. Certainly Blacks are not as represented in this exclusive group as they are in the general population but the increased income, property holdings and business equity propel many more of us over the threshold than before.

As a whole nation gets fed up with the nature of "corporate culture" and the means of purchasing business machinery becomes more affordable and available (computers, modems, printers, information storage capacity, etc.) more and more people are going into their own businesses.

In 1981 more people went into business than in any year in the history of America. It is through having one's own business, not through collecting a salary in a corporation, that people have chosen to grab their share of the nation's money. Again, as more Blacks realize this, the more "the market" rather than an all powerful White Employer will determine how much income they will have.

International business has skyrocketed in the last twenty years and the impact of economic interests in the Far East, Middle East and Europe is well known even to the man in the street. We can almost speak Japanese just by pronouncing the names of the stuff that we buy. White America has come to accept the idea of Third World People or People of Color who are rich, powerful and who impact not only in their own countries but help determine decisions in the U.S. as well. Many an American businessperson has come to the conclusion that the color of money is green. They could care less if it was a yellowish green, a whitish green or a very "dark" green as long as it was green. When former President Nixon, supposedly strongly anti-communist, visited China for trade inquiries in the 1970's, that eliminated the last nation from the list of places this country was *not* interested in trading with.

With all this having been said, it is still up to Black Americans, not anyone else, to decide *if* they want to make some money and how, when and where they are going to make this money. There may be a concept of quotas in some job categories but there will never be significant quotas in the world of business. We will get what we want when we decide we want it not when somebody decides to *give* it to us. It is important for Black Folks to understand that every single day, hundreds of millions of times a day, money changes hands with somebody giving it and somebody receiving it. With the exception of payday (twice a month) we are almost always the ones giving it. All we have to do is decide, plan for and make legitimate a vehicle for receiving money from anywhere in the world.

Attitude #6: I Don't Need Money to Enjoy Life (Money is Only For Material Things)

There are plenty of people who take the attitude that they don't need much money to enjoy a happy life because it is the simple pleasures in life that they enjoy the most. They believe that they don't need the big house on the hill, the fancy car, the flashy jewelry, fur coats or exotic vacations. Their thinking is that if they don't need the things that money buys, obviously, they don't need money either. After all, what is money for other than to spend? This line of thinking sounds rather sensible at first, especially if you have no personal craving for material things. As a matter of fact, this type of thinking even sounds healthy and refreshing considering the crass materialism that is fostered by television and the world in general. I personally accepted this line of thought as my own for many years.

But at a more critical and closer inspection this line of thinking is not healthy because it is limited, narrow and personal. Let me explain.

Black people have a well-known reputation as consumers. We buy virtually everything with our money. Many, many businesses count on us to buy their products if there is any hope of them making a profit. Black people do not save much of their money, but then Americans in general do not save much of their money as compared to people in other parts of the world. But the very last thing that Blacks do with their money is *invest it*. Investing is taking money that you don't need to spend and using it to *build something—anything*. Black people, unlike white people, limit their idea of the use of money to spending it on material goods as if that were the *only* thing that money was good for.

If you watch what rich people do with their money, you will see that they don't try to wear all of their money, or drive all of their money, or eat or drink or live in all of their money. What people with money do after they reach their level of material comfort (and often before they reach their level of comfort) is to invest their money in enterprises, ideas, organizations and institutions which have a meaning greater than their own personal life-style. There are over fourteen million businesses in this country and at least 96% are not owned by Blacks. A great deal of this nonmaterial money goes into the starting, building and strengthening of these businesses. Millions of dollars are used to develop colleges, museums, hospitals, charities, labor unions, political parties and political campaigns, research and exploration, etc. and etc. White America assumes the responsibility of developing next year's line of new cars, new fashions, new television programs and new computer technology.

Blacks, on the other hand, look at all these things as something that you simply consume. We don't save or borrow twenty-five million dollars to *develop* a computer, our job is to spend twenty-five hundred dollars to buy one once someone else (anybody but us) develops it and puts it on the market. This applies to auto cellular phones, microwave ovens, satellite dishes, everything. I hope you see the point.

Our attitude that our money or money in general is only to be used for our personal use items shows a distinct underdevelopment in the value and use of money. It also explains why our businesses are so under-financed because the idea of using our own money rather than a bank or S.B.A. Loan just never seems to enter our minds. This attitude has to change and quickly.

If there are to be significant increases in the number of services and goods we provide either to our people or to the world, we must understand that it will take a lot of money to develop the goods and services, to let people know about the existence of our goods and services and to deliver our goods and services. That is what all the other people in the world seem to be doing with their money.

In my mind, there is no person who cares about their family, community, race or nation who can really say that they don't need more money. They need it even if it's just to give it to someone or some institution that needs it more.

Attitude #7: Money Weakens Your Character, Makes You Soft and Spoils an Otherwise Good Human Being

This attitude of spoiling someone with money is again the product of the Black attitude of consumption. If all money was for was to spend on nice things to have, eat, wear or otherwise possess, then a person could get lazy and spoiled and unconnected to the real world if left a lot of money.

But if the attitude toward money is that it is simply a means with which to build something, then a person with money has more power or means to do something than someone who hasn't got any. The idea of money weakening one's character or making one soft or spoiled suggests that poverty would do the opposite. Does poverty strengthen one's Character? And what does strengthen mean; does it only mean one can physically fight better? I think the central point that people are alluding to in this relationship between money and character is the idea of *guts*. Can a rich man or woman have guts, bravery and be willing to respond to a challenge? We as Black people believe that the greatest challenge, the strongest character builder is to survive the ghetto, our own community. If a person can do that then they are supposedly of strong character. On the other hand, we believe that if a person does not grow up in the ghetto, does not have to struggle to survive because some parent or relative left them some money, property or business, then therefore they will not develop as strong a character or respond to the challenges the way our ghetto survivor would. Well I think that many of us are seeing only the narrow view of things just as we have in other areas.

There are many more ways to develop character and respond to challenges than simply making it in the dog-eat-dog world of the ghetto. Doesn't it take a lot of character to stand in the same spot for five hours and perform a heart transplant operation? Rich white boys from medical schools do that type of thing all the time.

Isn't it a challenge to take a half million dollar small company and in ten or fifteen years develop offices around the world?

We need to pass on money to our children so that they can play the game of life when they grow up. The greatest challenge, the greatest character builder is not surviving the ghetto but doing what everyone else in the world is doing and has done and that's making something out of nothing. Once upon a time McDonald's, Sears, Toyota, the Great Wall of China and the Pyramids were nothing. They did not exist. But they do today—because people and money made them exist. In the 1960's White America had to swallow a new definition of what a Black American (Negro) was. In the 1970's men had to swallow a new definition of what a female was. In the 1980's and beyond Black America has to come up with a different definition of what strong character is. It is not simply someone who survived hard times. It just as well could be someone who made good times even better.

Attitude #8: Religious and Political Fatalism

Oppressed people of all races and nationalities turn to many things to explain or tolerate their situations. If one can effectively discount the importance of what you don't or never will have, then it becomes a lot easier to live your life. Such tactics have been adopted by a significant and very vocal minority in the Black community who I refer to as "fatalists." There are basically two types of fatalists; religious and political. Although they may disagree on many things, they agree on at least one thing; it is completely unimportant to chase after the so-called almighty American Dollar.

The religious fatalist is a vocal personality who is constantly telling our people that the end of the world is near at hand and to prepare to meet the maker of the universe. Now, many religious bodies do believe in the eventual end of this world as we know it and that some type of judgment day will come. And while no one knows exactly when it is going to come (or, in fact, if it is really going to come) it has always been difficult for each generation to believe that it was due to happen in their particular lifetime. In any event, the religious fatalists would have us drop any pursuit of material gain immediately and simply wait for the end of the world. Wait, in other words, to die as we understand it. A surprising number of people do, in fact, embrace this idea; but it seems not coincidental that many of these believers are so near the poverty line already that they never really have to give up very much. I submit in all honesty that even if there was some reason to believe that the world was going to end during our lifetime, that we would still owe it to our family or parents and ourselves to provide the best that we could for all that we feel responsible for until that scary time actually came. And money would be a key item in being able to provide our loved ones with that type of care and protection. If I read between the lines and into the mind of the religious fatalists what they might be feeling, thinking and saying is this: "I'm so confused and totally off the mark at figuring out how to make it in this world that I'd like to see it end for everybody right now so that everybody will be as powerless to control their lives as I am right now."

The other kind of fatalist would be your political fatalist. A political fatalist is someone who may have adopted a Marxist or Socialist outlook and who is convinced that the American economic order is due to fall in a few short weeks. They have a disdain for people hustling for a buck, Black or White. These so-called political revolutionaries talk about the masses rising up and taking over the state. Many of the masses they are referring to can hardly rise up out of bed in the morning and take control over themselves. These Marxist preachings have been going on in this country for over a hundred years but there still is no problem getting a few recruits here and there to mouth the empty sayings. These revolutionaries have families and responsibilities like everyone else and they have to work somewhere to support themselves. You can usually find them working in community programs funded by foundation grants from the capitalists they supposedly hate (Ford, Rockefeller, Mellon, Carnegie, etc.). There are not a lot of fatalists among our people but the attitude of fatalism rears its head all too often and causes many people to never plan or act on their own ambitions or goals in life. This attitude, like the others, must be eliminated if our people are to develop the optimism that they will need to catch up.

Attitude #9: You Just End Up Paying More In Taxes

One of the absolutely discouraging things about studying the nature of Black Folks Problems is that you often haven't really done anything when you come up with an "answer" because the "answer" has a way of becoming a new problem. It's like a doctor who after listening to a patient's complaints recommends a cure only to find out that the patient refuses the cure. So, what has the doctor really done if he or she can't get the patient to take their medicine; it was a waste of time and expense for both of them.

I have heard Black Folks complain about their low salary on their jobs. But I have also heard some of these same people complain when getting more pay because they ended up paying more in taxes. How do you help a person who doesn't like where you found him but doesn't want to move either? Many poor people, and that includes a massive number of Black people, are what I call the H & R Block Short-Form Specialists. At tax time, they line up at these chain store-type accounting operations and sign the least detailed tax return that is available. Each has a gleam in their eye, hoping to get enough money back from the I.R.S. to purchase something that they weren't able to get at Christmas-time. Their understanding of receipts, deductions, write-offs and depreciation can be placed in one-half of a walnut shell. As far as they know the Government is all powerful in determining how much money they want and it's just nothing that they can do about it. Making money does not mean much to them because they believe there is no way that they could hold on to it even if they made it. Somehow they know that the rich seem to hold on to their money but they are always "too busy" to find out how they do it. Until somebody makes it easy and available and inexpensive for our people to understand how to save tax money, they will continue to pay maximum taxes. That is bad but not the worst. The worst is that we will continue to have thousands of people who will believe that it doesn't make *any difference* if you make more money or not. That would subject Black people for exploitation by everybody.

Attitude #10: I'm Too Old Now to Make Any Money

There are dozens of business magazines and newspapers on the market today that are filled with statistics. Among the statistics I remember reading was a profile of the so-called "typical" entrepreneur. As I recall, "he" was 32 years old, married with two children, owned his own home valued at about $72,000, and etc. The key thing that got my attention was the age. The article stated that at thirty-two years of age, new businessperson had at least ten years experience in the employee situation, had several promotions but had seen his (her) progress slow down a great deal and was now anxious to try to make it on their own. It is reasonable to assume that Black men are a bit older when they step out to do their thing, say 37 or so. In my own experience in traveling around the country, I have found the group in the mid-thirties to be the most interested and active in running their own businesses. But in the space of about eight years (45 years old or older) I have found a great number of men and women completely discount the idea that they could leave what they were doing to go into business. The greatest excuse that was always given was how close they were to collecting retirement or a pension. The second reason was that they had children in college, about to go to college or both. This one-two punch has knocked countless people out of considering starting a business. If I were to talk to a person of fifty and who could retire with benefits if they wanted to, and whose children were finished with school, they would most certainly say that they were too old and *mean* it. I will not suggest for a minute that starting or running an existing business is an easy thing to do. But when a person with fifteen good working years left in them pronounces that they are too old, it leaves you discouraged about the idea of Black folk ever catching up to where we should be in business. What this attitude means is that in an average Black person destined to live seventy or seventy-five years, they have only about ten years (between 32–42) to make a strong move to get into business. They are not going to get much encouragement from anyone to get started before then and they will have plenty of excuses (which everybody will accept) after that period of time.

I'd like to offer something to think about. Ray Kroc, the founder of McDonald's franchise concept, was *fifty-four* before he opened his *first* McDonald's. He died at nearly eighty, worth, according to some estimates, about a *billion dollars*! Colonel Harlan Sanders was sixty-five years old when the *Kentucky Fried Chicken* franchise concept began. He died at ninety, a multi-millionaire. I ask my "old" audience to raise their hands if they think they can make a hamburger at least as good as McDonald's or fry chicken at least as good as Kentucky Fried. The hands go up all over the room. I then ask people to look around the room and think about what they are saying.

Attitude #11: The Super Star Syndrome

I have made reference in other contexts to a concept I refer to as the "super star syndrome." I would like to take this opportunity to fully explain the concept here in order to shed some light on an anti-progressive attitude that exists in our community. The super star syndrome is very illustrative of the contradictory attitude that the Black community has about money and itself. Some background and detailed information is necessary to fully appreciate the situation.

Background

Shortly after the start of the 20th century, two developments were taking place simultaneously that were in a very real way opposite in nature.

One development was taking place in so-called "prestigious eastern universities" where "scholars" were starting two new fields of study called anthropology and sociology. These new fields were supposed to be more concentrated studies of the nature and evolution of man. At the center of these new studies were Black Americans. It seems that these scholars were trying to determine whether Black Folk were more man than animal or more animal than man. Specifically, it was assumed that we were somewhere along the gradual evolution of pure monkey to pure completed (European) man. This so-called scientific study gave good support to racists and Klu Klux Klaners who talked of race mixing causing mongrelization and keeping races pure, etc. In other words, the "educated" gave more reason for the ignorant to be ignorant.

The other development that was going on at the same time was that white businessmen, gamblers, promoters and the like were beginning to recognize Black men, and in some instances Black women, as athletes, artists and general entertainers. Although there was segregation, exploitation and racism for sure, there was no denial that the first Black Super Stars, such as boxer Jack Johnson and the early jazz artists and tap dancers etc., were being given privileged treatment and high salaries to perform for White only audiences. It was almost as if influential White Americans had held a conference and decided "these Blacks will be allowed special considerations as partial payment for their ability to perform and help us make money. The rest of the niggars will be held in check as usual." By the 1920's and 1930's there certainly appeared for the first time in significant numbers, Black entertainment stars. By the 1940's and 50's when the nation's sports teams desegregated, more Blacks chased the Jackie Robinson role model.

(By the 1960's the general Black public could eat and sleep in some of the places that Black stars could always enter, due to the broad power of the civil rights legislation of that period.)

In the 1940's and 50's the media began to emerge as the powerful tool it was to become. Black stars began to be covered on radio and occasionally on television. Black America, hungry for some form of acceptance by the majority population during these times (and constantly attempting to prove to the NATION that they were people and not animals) accepted virtually without question any personality that White America chose to accept. Eventually we made a decision with the Amos and Andy television show that we would start to become critical of the images being reflected back at us. When Nat "King" Cole won our first national television series opportunity, we thought we were on our way to acceptable role models. But as I speak to you there is still debate raging in our community about who does and who does not project a proper image of Black America to the rest of the nation and world. We debate if we should "tell it like it is" on the screen or whether we should project the way we would *like* to see it in the hope that television can speed on a new reality.

Today

If there was debate on the treatment of Black stars or their roles or their importance in the struggle for racial justice or any of a dozen other areas of theoretical and practical concern, there was one area that was not questioned. That area was *their right to the money that they earned.* Black people were always accepting of the great sums that Black athletes and entertainers earned. These great sums did not in general create any division, distance or jealousy between the star and their Black fans. As a matter of fact, because of the sums of money that our stars receive and because these sums are not a point of conflict or contention among our people, the stars experience a kind of freedom which is unique to our community in that their methods and intentions are rarely questioned or attacked. Unfortunately, it is a freedom which other members of our community are now allowed to enjoy. If our super stars want to move out of the Black community, marry across racial lines, send their kids to private schools or buddy up to the whitest richest members of corporate America, the Black community takes it all in stride. The stars suffer little criticism and hear few objections to almost anything that they do. Black people's attitude about stars is that they deserve all the money that they can get regardless of the sometimes mindless actions they perform to receive it. And secondly, they deserve to do with their money whatever they desire, though drug use is still frowned upon. The stars are the top, the cream, economically speaking, in our society.

The lower portion of our community, economically speaking, are the wage slaves. The overwhelming bulk of the people are tied to jobs they often hate at pay rates they consider inadequate. But they hang on and make the best of it and reward themselves with whatever lower level toys they can afford. America provides enough ways for them to escape a consciousness of their frustration that most problems are eventually resolved by simply reducing one's expectation of ones self and limiting one's dreams. Eventually the masses, at least the working masses, experience a kind of "freedom" in that they gradually come to terms with their station in life and no longer kick and scream for progress. The tension and stress that expectations create disappear. Most of us have the opportunity to march on with the rest of our lives at a leisurely pace.

Thus far, we have talked about two economic groups in our community; the stars at the top and the masses at the bottom portion of the spectrum. But there is a third group of Blacks which remain to be examined. This group is composed of Black business and professional people. They are an ambitious, talented, hardworking and educated group. And because of these characteristics, they are hassled. They are hassled for doing *the very same things* that the super stars do effortlessly and without comment. They are hassled for marrying across racial lines, hassled for sending their kids to private schools, hassled for moving out of the Black community and certainly chastized if they try to buddy up to the whitest, richest members of corporate America.

Everything that the Super Star can do without hassle and criticism, the Business and Professional Black has to do amidst hassle and criticism. Why is this?

Well, I believe it is because the Black community doesn't really believe the professional Black deserves what they have. They believe the successful Black was just lucky, or had connections or is simply ripping off the masses. Anything is used to try to explain that their success is due to everything but hard and smart work.

What I'm essentially saying is that Black folk are prejudiced and believe in privileged classes among their own people. They have two sets of standards—one for the super star and one for everybody else. To my knowledge, we are the only people in America that does not believe that all of us should live good if we can legitimately make it. This, Folks, is probably the most self-defeating and anti-money attitude that we have. It makes ambitious people have to stop and think about whether they want to be successful or if they want to keep their old friends. Somehow, to have both seems improbable.

I have studied this concept for a long time to try to detect what specific thing separates a super star from the rest of us crabs in the barrel. Essentially, it is just one thing—White Approval, or, more specifically, White *Media* Approval. White approval has always influenced how (or if) we approved of ourselves. This is part of our heritage, unfortunately. But with the tremendous rise of the power of television, cable and media in general, white opinion has taken on new meaning. Media visibility translates today as White acceptance. The more powerful the media (the movie screen is still #1 in power) the greater is the assumed acceptance. The media magnifies every good aspect and hides every negative aspect of the star. With a bigger than life image, and universal appeal, the general public has no reason to believe anything other than that the person must be great, and must be worth the attention and praise being given them. What else are they to think? And if they have made it and travel the nation and the world, then they must rightly *deserve* all the money that is coming in from all these parts of the world. The bottom line is that the Black community (as does the White community) accepts their stars because they are *programmed* to accept them. It is very important to note that most of this money is coming from the white owners of athletic teams, record companies, movie studios, etc. Thus, from the Black community's point of view, Black stardom in most cases is all gain and at very little cost to the community.

The story in regards to Black business and professional people is very different however. The Black professional and business person seldom get access to the all-powerful media. As far as media is concerned, the only Blacks worthy of their attention are athletes and entertainers. Due to the nature of the work of lawyers, doctors, accountants, etc., glamorizing is difficult. The public cannot learn from the media why a particular Black professional or lawyer is so great, unique, valuable, etc., if media chooses not to cover these types of stories. At this point, it is important to understand that Black media (magazines, newspapers, radio stations and television programs) have a tendency to both highlight and ignore the same types of personalities that White media selects. Black media has not been the instrument of projecting alternative role models for the Black community that it could have been. With no press, representatives or hype to design their image, the Black business and professional person's value and image is to be directly interpreted by the public they serve. It is here that the many differences and conflicts arise.

First of all, unlike the situation with the Black superstar that is making millions of dollars a year, money differences and lifestyle difference do cause a distance to develop and grow between Black business people and professionals and the masses. With superstars, their money comes from white owned companies (even though millions of Blacks buy the records and attend the concerts, games and shows), whereas with the Black business and professional group the money comes from the hands of the clients directly into the till of the professional. This gives the Black public more justification to be critical, perhaps, since the contacts are so direct. The wealth of the Black business person is seen as being a direct cost to the community, rather than a gain in community income coming from the outside White world. Now, the community feels if you are going to become wealthy from their hard-earned dollars, then you are going to have to give back to the community. Obviously, each business and professional person responds in his or her own way; some giving a great deal and some giving virtually nothing. Some are very quiet with their giving and the public never even knows while others like to see their picture in the paper handing over the check to the recipient. But just as a fool can ask more questions than a wise man can answer, a beggar can ask for more than a wealthy person can give. So many people in the Black community have their hands out begging for their endless causes that the small entrepreneurial group in our community could never afford to give back to the community the amount of money the community thinks they should contribute. I think this adds to the friction between the two "classes."

In the minds of the Black business and professional persons a series of frustrating circumstances cause a build-up of resentment against the masses. For one, the masses continually expect service whether they have the money (or even the *intention to pay*) or not. The masses don't seem to feel guilty for not paying the doctor, lawyer, dentist or accountant. They assume professionals are already doing ok ("they won't even *miss* my money"). Obviously, this can cripple any type of operation if enough people fail to pay. It's curtains if you get a reputation as a "softee" on debt collection and credit. The Black professional also gets frustrated by the fact that the masses have very little appreciation for the work, money, sacrifice, and pressure that the business and professional person has had to go through to get whatever they've obtained. The fees and profits aren't there to necessarily finance a yacht; they are there to pay back tremendous school loans, special equipment loans and ongoing rent and overhead costs. But because the Black community knows so little about the details of business, this goes over their heads. It is also very common for the masses to attribute the success of a business and professional person to "luck." This, I think, really hurts anyone who has worked hard for what they've earned. Rather than being viewed with a certain amount of awe (which does, in fact, happen occasionally) the successful Black is too often viewed with a certain amount of resentment ("the lucky bastard; why couldn't it have been me; when am I going to get a break"). Finally, the Black business and professional person feels, in a sense, always out front, being watched and analyzed and bound by the image of their profession or business. The freedom that financial success was to give them can really only be exercised if they get away from the eyes, ears, judgments and criticisms of those that are quick to dictate role model behavior. For that reason, it is only natural why successful Blacks would move out of poorer communities. Unlike the interpretation with Black superstars, when Black business and professional people move to richer, suburban communities, it is considered a genuine form of desertion and naturally this brings on another level of jealousy, misunderstanding and friction between the two groups.

To summarize the purpose and meaning of this attitude once again: Black people have historically, and unfortunately, adopted the same standard as Whites in terms of deciding who in the Black community deserves to make money and have the freedom of choice and lifestyle that is to come with money. Whites have basically limited their concept of a "rich Negro" to athletes and entertainers because it is in their best interests to pay Black talent as important members of their own sport and entertainment business empires.

The Black community does not feel comfortable that Blacks not projected, supported and paid by the White community should come into their own communities and accumulate wealth, regardless of the service they are offering. Should Black business and professional people successfully accumulate wealth from the community (by the provision of their services), the dominant feeling in the community is that significant and consistent demands should be placed on that Black achiever. The demands appear over and above normal. The Black community does not conceive or consider the idea that these demands or expectations are an infringement on the freedom of the Black business and professional person. The Black business and professional person often is put on the defensive on each and every point.

I have devoted considerable effort to explain our negative financial-social situation. I have done so because I am fearful of what I have seen and continue to see and that is the ever-widening gap between the Black "haves" and the Black "have-nots." Class division is moving rapidly in our community and is largely due to this terrible confusion among us as to where money comes from, how it is acquired, who deserves it and what you can do with it once you get it. Obviously, you don't spend it all but then you don't give it all away either. Unfortunatley, there is no organized effort going on in the Black community to discuss this confusion so the division and misunderstandings continue. I see wealthy Blacks spending thousands of dollars in home, car and business alarm systems to prevent them from being ripped off by poorer Blacks. I see each group wishing to live further away from the other. It is the most unhealthy thing going on in our community.

Summary on Personal Attitudes

It is important for me to repeat over again (for some people I can't repeat it often enough) that many races and cultures of people in the U.S. (and outside of it) share some of the same hangups, problems, confusions and attitudes about money as Black Americans. That to me is not the issue. The issue is, how can we as a people improve our financial condition, period! This issue is how much *more* do *we* suffer the problems than other people. The issue is, can you feel comfortable in running the same speed as everyone else if you need to catch up.

Business people are individual community members who have had just as much exposure to these self-defeating money attitudes as anyone else. Many of these business people have no more success getting rid of their anti-money hangups as regular, salaried people. Often these business people are not aware that unconsciously they are uncomfortable with the idea of having a lot of money. But this is all part of the reason *why Black Businesses are the way they are*. They are the way they are partly because the individual owners are not interested in making a lot of money because they, like most Blacks, don't believe they can do it, should do it or even deserve to have a lot of money. What many of them are secretly saying to themselves is, "Why should I expect to ever have money? Who am I? I'm nobody special. I'm just like everybody else and it's very important that everybody else thinks that I'm just like them." Though Black businesspersons take more risks and work longer hours, many believe they really shouldn't have any more than anybody else.

Let me ask you a question. Where do you think the inventors of the

Hula Hoop, or the Pet Rock, or Rubic's Cube or Trivial Pursuit would be if they thought like that? Would they be multimillionaires and in control of their lives if they thought they didn't deserve to reap the profit of the one idea they had in their lives?

Black businesses are the way they are partly because the owners do not expect to do any more than get by. So what you see when you walk in the door all too often is whatever the owner thinks will "get by." The equipment, the products, the facility and the service may be inadequate but in the minds of the owners, *it will get by.* And if Black customers do not expect or demand better products or services from their businesses, the business owner is *absolutely right.* He or she is *getting by and getting over.*

Black Business Attitudes

Up to this point, we have been analyzing negative money attitudes that dominate the minds of the entire community. Unless you have been completely isolated from the Black church, your grandparents, your parents, your teachers, etc., you have heard and been nurtured in most of the attitudes listed above. I wish I could say that these attitudes were our only hurdle.

But I am afraid that this is not the case. Because after we finish understanding the various personal attitudes, we have to analyze our Business attitudes. After all, if Black people don't go into business to make a lot of money then they must have other reasons . . . right? They must approach business with their own unique set of attitudes if their attitude is not the old standard, "I'm gonna be a millionaire" approach.

That is specifically what we are going to examine right now. What are the reasons that many Blacks go into business if not for economic prosperity? Let us begin.

Reason #1: To Be the Boss

Black people have historically been slaves, laborers and workers. There has always been a White overseer, bossman, foreman or supervisor looking over our shoulder to see if we were doing the job they wanted, the way they wanted us to do it. It's not surprising that a certain portion of this working class, both male and female, become fed up with this routine and start their own business—to be free from the hassle of a "boss." There is nothing inherently wrong with this feeling. But too often this new businessperson has a life-long chip on their shoulder and they now substitute their own tyrant-like ways in place of the supervisor they have just left. In other words, these business people need to show everybody that enters their place of business that they are the boss and they are in control. This seriously affects their ability to be friendly, courteous and serve the people. Instead, customers pick up a kind of hostility, disagreeableness or apathy almost from the moment they enter the establishment. Many of these types of businesspeople could not possibly view themselves as servants of the public or as having a responsibility to the public. As a matter of fact, the attitude of a "Me Boss Man" type of owner is almost the opposite of a money-minded business owner. For example:

Money-Minded Owner	Boss Man Owner
Greets customers with a smile whether they feel good or not.	May or may not greet customer depending on how they feel.
I must prove to the people that we are the best, the friendliest, cleanest, the cheapest, etc.	I ain't got to prove a damn thing to anybody. Those days are over.
The customer is always right.	If you don't like it, you can leave now and you don't have to come back in here anymore.
I must set an example for my employees and not ask them to do anything I can't do.	If they don't do like I tell 'em I'll fire 'em; simple as dat.

The bottom line consideration for this type of business owner is control. He (sometimes, she) is more interested in feeding their ego than their pockets. All their working lives they have been walked on. This time, they are going to do the walking. But the public doesn't have to tolerate rudeness if they don't want to and very often this type of business person is soon out of business. That's what happens when customers won't come in your store anymore. But to hear our disgruntled business owner tell it, it was all the Black customers' fault that they didn't support him. From his point of view, they should have supported him just because he was Black, and service didn't have anything to do with it. Chalk up another dead business.

Reason#2: For Prestige

The second reason that many Blacks seek to go into business is the desire for prestige. As employees, there is often a very limited amount of status associated with the work that Blacks can attain. Therefore, in order to elevate themselves in status, some seek business ownership and preferably a business that itself carries a certain amount of status. Again, there is nothing wrong, as I see it, with this perspective of business owner- ship if it doesn't color sound financial decisions. But a person seeking status is often investing money in *looking the part of success*. They often withdraw from the the real nitty-gritty, nuts and bolts aspect of their business. In a business, the key to success is sacrifice, living below your means and reinvesting profits back into the business. This is against the grain of your status-oriented businessperson. They want to bask in their glory *today*. The unwise financial decisions that often follow this attitude is usually the direct cause of the business's failure.

It must also be mentioned that status or prestige-oriented businesspeople often turn their backs on real money-making opportunities if such oppor- tunities lack prestige. For example, on a main street in a predominantly Black major city, you may have two businesses for sale. One is a laundro- mat which is very crowded most days and can be very profitable if the owner wears overalls and fixes the machine break-downs himself. The other business for sale is an art gallery-antique shop which simply was not of interest to the local residents. The prestige-oriented businessperson will turn his back on the laundromat even if the business is making a kill- ing, because the situation lacks the status that he is seeking. What he might try to do is think of a way to spark interest in art and antiques in the neighborhood because that business does have a certain amount of "class" associated with it. Thus, money is definitely not the motivation for this person.

The prestige-oriented business owner has a variety of popular sayings and rationales that they can hide behind to explain or justify their attitude and/or behavior. For example, if they are spending their money as fast (or faster) as they are making it, it wouldn't be considered playing a role; they would just say, "You've got to look successful to be successful." And with that one cute cliché (which is true only occasionally) they can spend themselves into the next century. Another popular statement is "Money draws Money"—meaning, I guess, if you look rich, rich people will be drawn to you (and, we are to assume, give you some of their money). I'm not saying that there are not dozens of people who could testify that this philosophy has worked for them, but I'll bet you ten times that number could say that the obsession with status and the *appearance of substance* led them into business problems or business failure. The least prestigious thing a person could do is to have all their precious belongings auctioned off for pennies on the dollar and start life over yet another time. A word to the wise.

Reason #3: For Fun and Hobbies

The desire for fun through the development of a hobby pushes a certain sector of our community into business. The "hobbyist" is a person who has gained a skill and has earned some money on the side by marketing their skills to friends, family and acquaintances. The idea dawns on them to do the enterprise full-time because he or she envisions a situation of earning a living doing the thing that they love to do anyway. The driving force in this business attempt is not money, power, bossism or prestige; it is the desire to simply put a fuller commitment into something that you are happy with and accomplished at doing. In the white world, thousands of people have gone to make millions by simply doing what they like to do because a market was found for the talent, whatever it was. But in the world of Black America, where our business friend would *probably* have to start—the question that has to be asked is, will this hobby, will this fun thing to do, earn enough to pay the overhead, expenses and return a liveable profit? *That question is often not asked!* Our hobbyist plunges in and takes the ultimate risks. Sometimes they bloom and become nationally known. Too often, however, our hobbyist closes up shop too soon after opening and is left with a sense of disappointment and apathy.

The problem in this instance often lies in the fact that the hobbyist has underestimated the importance of understanding the details of business—of making money. A hobbyist usually has to be backed by a financial person.

A financial person has to add to the business the money-making concern and money management thinking that the hobbyist doesn't bring to the business. When this fails to happen the business usually fails to happen.

It's my belief that it is this sector of the Black business community that holds the most promise for our people. When you have people who like to do something, are good at it and are willing to put in long hours without immediate concern with jumping into a lavish lifestyle, you have the making of a potential dynamite business person. We have people like this, thousands of them. What we don't have enough of are business minds (White, Black or Oriental) who are willing to take time with these people and guide their careers and develop their markets. I mentioned before the items of Hula Hoops, Rubic's Cube and Trivial Pursuit. Understand that nobody in the world *needs* a Hula Hoop or Rubic's Cube, but that doesn't mean that the market couldn't be developed for the product. I'm not suggesting Black talent should develop worthless items for the sake of money; what I am saying is that a businessperson can develop a market for just about any interesting product, whether it is specifically *needed* or not. Where are these Black marketing people you ask? Well, right now they are on a plane for Dallas, Texas, where they are to attend a marketing seminar for their company—IBM, XEROX, General Motors, or AT&T. Our best Black business minds are helping White corporations make even more money. (More on that later.) The bottom line here is this—business should be enjoyable, especially if you intend to put in the required hours and develop an appreciation for what you are doing. But fun is of no use if it makes no financial sense. That is what many of us have been doing, failing to successfully negotiate the financial wall. In many instances, it can be done, but we as Black people are going to have to bring more to the negotiating table than what we've been bringing so far. *Pure hobbies* are different from pure business and are best left at home.

Reason #4: For Community Service/ Non-Profit(able) Enterprises

Have you ever noticed that the closer you get to the poorest parts of the ghetto, the more *non-profit* programs you begin to see? Non-profit housing, non-profit food co-op, non-profit theatre company and so on. This is an example of the Poverty Program gone mad. Why is it that everybody in the world is making money building houses, selling food and displaying art and yet we are supposed to do it for free.

I believe it goes back to the anti-business mood of our Black leadership in the 1960's (I know you younger readers get sick and tired of hearing about the '60's, but believe me, brothers and sisters, it was very, very different from today).

Government and foundation grants were there for the asking—so we asked, and we asked. Many of us never realized that we were becoming a foundation junkie who needed a "foundation grant fix" to keep his or her program going. That, in my mind, is what appeared to have happened. We played right into the hands of White America. The way we saw it in the 60's was very simple. If we "took" (accepted) the White man's money, it was a politically progressive act, it was reparation money that was "owed us" for all the free labor that our ancestors gave this country. But if we set out to make a profit, actually run things like a business, then that was a politically unprogressive act because that was capitalistic, exploitive and opportunistic. So this was the line of reasoning that we followed and White folks loved it because they controlled everything. They controlled how much money would be allocated and for what programs and how long the funding would last. Meanwhile, they controlled our will and desire to work for ourselves; which was the tragic part of it. Finally, if there were any explosions of anger or vindictiveness, we would only burn down our own neighborhoods anyway.

Although I think I understand a great part of this, I am still rather ashamed that our so-called leaders at the time couldn't see what was happening. In all fairness, I must say that during this time there was one national leader, The Honorable Elijah Muhammad, who was constantly pushing the concept of "Do for Self," but too many people could not hear that message because they allowed other ideas of the man to obscure their objectivity.

The legacy of nonprofit economic development (a greater contradiction in terms in inconceivable) is with us today. There are still "special programs" that Blacks stand in line for and they have done some good for thousands of people. But the cost of the programs on our people is staggering; we lost *half a generation* of business growth because some figureheads (both Black and White) convinced twenty million people that you could have economic development without making money.

How has this affected the attitudes of our people? Well, many thousands of our people grew up thinking that the government's (Federal, State, County and City) role was to provide jobs for everyone, which is obviously impossible. To many White bureaucrats, the money was give-away money where nothing was really *expected* to happen. Nothing was to be really *produced* or *sold* and record-keeping as we know it was often a joke. Even the least aware teenager knew that the real purpose of a lot of the money was to keep "cool heads" in the community. It was anti-riot money and it shot up a great deal in July and August and was gone by October.

When many Blacks who came up through this eventually did get *real* jobs in schools, fast food restaurants, hospitals, the military, etc.; they treated those positions as if they were still working for the poverty program. That attitude has and still is hurting us in business. I know of no nation in the world nor any people in the world that would respect us as business people as long as we beg for our money and say we are a nonprofit people.

"Profitable" Community Service

There are many community-minded people who have a history of involvement with various programs, city agencies, etc., who have left these places to start their own thing. Many of these people have seen in practice what we are talking about here—the waste, the dependency, the poor follow-up on problems, etc. So, as their personal response to the situation, they decide to try to continue their service and commitment to their people but in the confines of their own enterprise. This is all well and good. The problem comes in when that person, in developing their new enterprise, doesn't take the time or interest to learn about business and run his/her activities accordingly. The idea of profit is not only ignored but many of these people have been heard to brag, "I'm not in this for the money; if I wanted to make some real money I could be doing this or that" (actually it's always debatable if they could move into a profitable situation as quickly as they would have us think). The community service person still runs their "new" enterprise very much with the spirit if not the techniques of a non-profit outfit. They find it easier to give than to sell because selling is still not registering as serving. They also find it difficult to sell because the people they are relating to many times expect to be given to ("Is this free?" they ask). I want to make it clear that this is not a lower class phenomenon. If you ever attend the large national conventions of our major civil rights organizations, you will find thousands of our middle class representatives grabbing all the "freebies" that the major corporations are giving away. In most cases, *selling* is not even allowed; things *must* be given away. It wouldn't be any big thing, really, if it did not remind me so vividly of the mentality of our people.

As an author, book writer-publisher, I deal with many Black bookstores. (Bookstores are a common place that the community-minded activist gravitates to in terms of doing their own thing.) In many instances, these bookstores are fine examples of business enterprises who unfortunately are losing profits because of the decay of our schools, the obsession with television and the whole movement away from reading going on at all levels in the U.S. But many other bookstores were obviously never set up to make money in the first place. You can tell by their hours, their limited inventories and their lack of marketing and promotion. Many operate more like secret societies rather than public places. And they pay bills without any consideration of credibility, future credit allowances or reputation. They do not deal with the fact that heat, rent, shipping, taxes, labor, etc., all have to be paid out of the profits they don't seem to care about. Sometimes I find that they go out of business and rather than be surprised, I wonder how they were able to hang on so long.

The point in this example is that there is nothing wrong with serving the community. Businesses should serve the community. But if you do not run your business like a business and make money as a business should, then you will soon be out of business. Being out of business would disappoint and be inconvenient to all the people you were trying to serve and your business would be a new example of how Black businesses fail. And that would be a disservice to the people you are trying to serve.

Reason #5: Convenience

There are a lot of similarities between the "Me Bossman" motivation of going into business and the person who goes into business with the idea of convenience. The convenience-oriented businessperson is tired of the hassles on the 9–5 job routine and they go into business not to ego-trip but because they want an easier life. They are tired of the twin identities that they are living (one on the job—one at home). They just want to *relax* so they start one of the most challenging things one can do (starting a business) in order to relax.

This is the kind of person whose shop hours are supposed to start at 9 a.m. but they actually open up at 10 a.m. (it's more convenient that way). They are suppoed to close at 6 p.m. but after you break your neck to get there at 5:30 p.m., you see that they are already closed anyway. This owner leaves a cardboard clock on their front door saying they will be back in ten minutes, or at 1 p.m., and you blow your whole lunch-hour waiting for them to return. When you enter their store, they don't stop reading their newspaper or pop up out of their chair to serve you. They may ask, "Can I help you," without budging one muscle in their body. I think most of you have met this type of person. If you like him or her you call them "easy-going"—if you don't like them, you might call them a "lazy S.O.B."

This business is set up with one basic thing in mind. It is not profit, customer service or community service. It is set up so that everything is convenient for the owner, period! As a matter of fact, the owner dreams of the day when he or she doesn't even have to be there to do anything. But their profits are so low that they will never be in a position to hire anybody so they are stuck there. Their place of business in their mind is not really a place of business but their living room. You might find them with their slippers on, smoking and watching a cartoon show or the soaps. If you stretched your imagination, could you understand why this person is not making any money and why one day they might not have to ever leave their living room for real?

Reason #6: To Get Over

The Black entrepreneur whom I classify as the one who starts a business to "get over" does not start out that way. This point is very important to keep in mind if you are to understand this personality and what it says about our way of thinking. The "get over" business person is often a highly educated, sophisticated and confident person. This male or female takes a corporate job (usually) after some form of rather impressive college education. This shining Black star rises up through the ranks and for a while is doing every bit as well as the Whites with similar backgrounds and training. All is well for a while. Then in some middle management position seven years down the road, our friend here gets stuck in a position that seems to hold them like quicksand. They can't complain about racism because others seem to be stuck also. The salary they are receiving is rather nice (between 30–40 thousand a year) and, of course, the benefit package and general working atmosphere is great. But the loss of momentum, the feeling of forward progression and advancement has stopped. After a couple of years of looking to relocate, our corporate star starts to really get frustrated and begins to seriously, for the first time in his or her life, think about starting their own business and making some "real" money. Then one day their supervisor (corporate personnel never have "bosses") in a conversation says something that made it all click. The supervisor's statement suggested that there would be *no further promotions* to speak of. The suggestion was that the Black corporate star had, in fact, reached the level of responsibility that the corporation felt was within their means to handle. In fact, the supervisor thought that our employee here knew that or had "put that together." In other words, our future entrepreneur is being told, "I hope you are happy where you are, buddy, because this is about as far as you can expect to go."

Well, that set of circumstances becomes the thing that propels our Black businessperson out of the corporate world and into the world of small business.

After hard planning, sacrifice, hard work, and all the other dues that must be paid to have a successful enterprise, our bright businessperson is rolling along nicely. They have a good reputation and everything is great. But then, at about the time our friend here reaches the point where they are making about $40,000 a year, things slow down. Like the corporate situation, the forward movement stops. The question you might ask is "Why?" Well, every case is different, that's quite clear, but I have a theory that I've reached after talking to and reading about hundreds of people. The theory is this. Whenever anybody sets out on a project, they usually have set some type of goal or set of goals. Among these goals are *minimum goals, basic goals* and *ultimate goals*. Obviously, different people have varying degrees of realism or ambition in their goal-setting. But, somewhere in this mixture of goals, you pass over a success threshold. If you reach that one goal, you consider yourself a winner and if you fall short, you might feel somewhat like a failure. *Many people never expect to fail in attaining their minimum goals and never really expect to actually reach their ultimate goals.* Success is somewhere in the middle. But where? Well, in the case of Black America, we reject the idea of Whites constantly feeling like they are in a position to evaluate us and our value (in this case, 30–40 thousand a year). However, many of us believe much of what White folks say because they are always in control, either teaching us, testing us, "allowing" us to work with them or for them and generally running the country and half the world. We end up believing whatever they say even if it is about ourselves. So what happens is this: if White folks say that we are worth $40,000 a year and we start our own business, that $40,000 figure becomes our definition of success. In many of our hearts, we believe, "If I can make as much in my own thing as I can working for THE MAN, then I'm successful." Of course, our ultimate goal may be to double our old salary ($80,000 a year). But as I said, most people never expect or design their plans to reach their ultimate goals. They don't consider not reaching their ultimate goal as *failure*. Also, they don't set their absolute minimum goal as matching their old salary either. If that is the most money they ever made in their lives, it is very unlikely that they are going to say, "I'm going to make the most money I ever made to be my minimum goal." That just doesn't seem practical or possible. So what happens is that a person passes their minimum goal and never reaches their ultimate goal and is doing as well financially as they ever did, on their own. They have to call themselves a success. When people (running, politics, acting—it doesn't matter) reach what they consider a success, they usually slow down. When you are in your own business and you slow down and you are Black and serve mostly Black people, believe me, your business and its profits will begin to slow down also.

Now, let's look at this situation again to point out the contradictions clearly. First, of all, the motivation for this person to go into business was to get more money than what the corporation was willing to pay. The important consideration in looking at this thing is not how much the

Black person is making in their business but how much more they are making in relation to the value that White folks put on them. If I run into a sister or a brother who is making $75,000 a year in their own business, I am impressed. But If I find out that they were making $65,000 at some major corporation, three, four, five years before, I lose a bit of my appreciation for the achievement. Unless we really pay ourselves an income and benefit package that surpasses what any person could reasonably believe that their former employer would have paid them, then we are really not in business to make money; we are just in it to get over with the same lifestyle we could have had anyway and without the risk. I am not saying, I repeat, I am not saying it is not better to work for yourself and maintain your lifestyle; I believe it is. But I also believe it is good to not lie to one's self and to be very clear with where your head really is.

Summary of Black Business Attitudes

Now, what I have tried to illustrate in these last pages is that Black Business people's motivation for going into business is too often not related to making money or profits. Yet it is making money or profits that will determine if your business ceases or continues, succeeds or fails. Too often when a business fails, the Black businessperson will immediately blame other Black people for not supporting him or her, when, in fact, the business operation was never designed to cater specifically to the needs of the customers in the first place. And if you have a business that does not cater to or address the needs of customers, then it should be no surprise whatsoever that you have less customers and therefore less money. Usually when I point out these concepts to groups I am "attacked" for overgeneralizing. So many people are quick to point out the exceptions rather than the rule that I must do this. Am I saying that all Black businesspeople have these negative attitudes? No, they do not. But far too many businesses do have these problems and they need to be told so they can look at themselves and decide what they want to do.

Am I saying that White-owned businesses are free from these hangups and that, therefore, these problems are only a Black problem? No, I am not saying that either. There are about 14 million businesses in the nation and about 3% of them are Black-owned. White businesses could suffer from the problems discussed three times worse than Black businesses and that wouldn't change the fact that Black Americans do not control the economics of their community. We simply have such a task ahead of us that we cannot afford to tolerate whatever problems we have if they can be identified and eliminated. If you are not with me here, you probably will miss the point of the whole book.

The Development of Customer Expectations

It has been mentioned previously that prior to the desegregation of America, Black people were basically forced to patronize their own businesses. During this long period of time, we as a people operated on a survival strategy; do whatever had to be done to make it. There was anything but consistency in our lives; each month and year brought new conditions which in turn demanded new adjustments. It would have been rather unrealistic for Black people to have a set of business expectations under these circumstances. When we walked into our brothers' and sisters' establishments, we accepted whatever we found and paid whatever was reasonable. As a matter of fact, the gracious customers would bend over backward to make everyone connected with a local business feel that they were comfortable in the most makeshift of situations. Everyone seemed to want to be the first to say, "They didn't need much to get by." But times soon changed.

With integration came the opportunity for Blacks to see how the other folks had been living all the time. As barrier after barrier came down and we began to understand the true meaning of "shopping," "night out on the town," and "pick and choose," we developed the idea of standards and expectations. Whereas before in the South we seldom expressed disappointment, today we are quick to express dissatisfaction with less than expected standards or service. It is very important to make a careful distinction between complaining out of a type of self hate and the evolution of ones standards. People grow. Let's take, for example, the idea of a restaurant. Restaurants are a highly competitive business since everyone eats and a higher proportion of our people are eating away from home an increasing number of times. Many Black customers have grown to expect the following:

— a parking space for their car and that space to be paved and well lit;

— to be seated at a table and met by a friendly, clean waitress who is taking her time to wait *on them*;

— to be able to make special requests about how they would like their food and that the food will arrive within a reasonable amount of time;

— that the restaurant be very clean, neat and attractively decorated;

— the absence of insects, smoke, odors, loud noise, loud talk, other irritants;

— that efforts will be made to please them, cheerfully, if they are not satisfied with their food;

— that the waitress will return to their table after their food has been served to see if there is another request or service needed;

— that special considerations can be or are made for children and/or large groups;

— that the establishment will honor any of a number of credit cards as payment for their meal.

Now, these are the things that a typical person, Black or White, who goes to a restaurant has grown to expect. They expect it because they have received the same treatment so many times that well, like I said, they expect it. The only issue for them is the quality of the food and the prices. Everyone reading these expectations has received them many times in the various places they have eaten. But how many of you have received all of them from a Black restaurant? Even in major cities it is difficult to find Black restaurants that have their own parking lot or that accept credit cards—a standard business/social instrument. The point is that the people who are Black who have the money to make your business successful have expectations about how your business is to be run. It is much more important that you meet those expectations than to prove that you are the boss doing your own thing. The same set of principles could apply to just about any business. Customers have expectations. Good Black Business dictates that you can determine what the reasonable expectations are for your type of business. Do not assume, as so many always do, that "you ain't got to do all that for Black Folk. This is a 'Grass Roots Joint' here." Of course, there are all too many Grass Roots Joints—here, there, everywhere. What we need are sound places of business.

The issue that glares out at you when discussing this point is, "should a Black person support another Black business . . . regardless of whether it meets standards or not? Should you support it just because it is Black, period."

People are very good at giving good reasons for being on either side of this issue. I *don't* believe you should buy from a Black person just because they are Black and I will tell you why. When you "buy Black" regardless of circumstances, you are excusing Blacks from the very function of business which is to please customers. You do not create stronger businesses by excusing the business owner from the responsibility and challenge of business; what you are doing is insuring a second-class, or third-class, business will stay alive when maybe it should not. Maybe if that business went out of business a better business could be brought to life and learn from the mistakes of the former enterprise. In other words, you are helping defeat the purpose of developing sound, strong Black businesses if you allow weak and unresponsive businesses to thrive—just because they are Black.

The BLACK Brain Drain

In the early part of this century, W.E.B. DuBois (probably the greatest Black intellectual of this century) coined a concept called the "talented tenth" theory. This idea stated that all people are led by the intellectuals that develop among them and that these thinkers, scientists, artists, explorers, etc., comprise the top 10% of any particular people. And it was the responsibility of these gifted people to come up with the answers for the problems of the other 90% of the people and lead the entire mass of people to progress. DuBois, a Harvard-trained PhD graduate of 1899 did, in fact, dedicate all of his life to helping Black Americans and encouraging other Black intellectuals to do the same. During his time (up to 1963), Black thinkers had, in fact, *little choice* but to relate to the Black community because the White community *did not want them*. DuBois, even with his PhD, could hardly have been expected to be hired by Mellon Bank or Ford Motor Company or any of the developing White financial empires of the day because they weren't hiring Blacks, *period*, regardless of what they had to offer. There was no alternative left but to serve one's people, unless one when off to Europe which a few Black writers and thinkers did, in fact, do.

Today, however, we have gone very much in the opposite direction. Rather than talented Black people working for the community's improvement, they are standing in line to submit their résumés to IBM, XEROX, Mobil Oil, Gulf and Western, etc. I call this phenomenon the "Black Brain Drain," meaning, of course, that the brainy or highly educated or specially talented folks in the Black community are not pouring these talents into their community but, rather, that those talents are being *drained away* from the community to serve other interests. This is an extremely important thing to examine and it relates very much to trying to get an understanding of why Black businesses are the way they are.

If we want a clear picture of what has and is happening, we have to see it in some type of historical context. W.E.B. DuBois was one of the founding members of the N.A.A.C.P. Whereas DuBois was very much a leader in terms of Black people serving Black people, the N.A.A.C.P. has had a long history in having integration as a working philosophy. After 45 years of struggle (the N.A.A.C.P. was founded in 1909), the legal support for integration came with the 1954 court decision mentioned earlier. Integration of schools led to the push for integration in everything. Corporations with their millions of jobs were definitely a target on the agenda of integrationists. With law, M.B.A. and other specialized degrees, Blacks did in fact begin to filter into the formerly all-White, mostly male corporations. The reasons that there was no suspicion on the part of Black America that this may not be a good thing is due to the fact that corporate employment seemed to answer everyone's needs, if not dreams. Black parents felt pride in seeing their children go to work in a suit rather than overalls and that they worked in clean, safe places rather than factory sweatshops. The parents could see that one day their child might supervise some White folks rather than always being supervised by them. The long hours of scrubbing floors and pinching pennies was being paid off by these choice corporate placements.

The government could feel happy because maybe the Black protesting and rioting would stop if the leadership strata of Blacks could be placed in jobs that weren't frustrating or undignified. All government officials would have preferred not to watch looting, burning and shooting on the 6 and 11 o'clock newscasts.

The Black graduates were happy not just because they could see the pride and happiness on their parents' faces but because they were proud themselves. After all, if you are measured by White standards from grades 1 through 12 and then, four or five years of college, you wanted to believe that you measured up to the standard in the end at the place it mattered most—the workplace. Obviously, the appeal of substantial salaries and benefits would be a great payoff for them personally since the school experience was a substantial struggle. The moral consciousness of Black graduates said also that Black youth needed role models and there was always the historical burden of "representing the race."

Finally, millions of White liberals who had fought and pushed as protesters, boycotters, sit-in-ers, lawyers, judges, philanthropists, etc., had a stake in all this too. They had a vision of an unwaveringly fair country that would not judge people on the basis of race, religion or natural origin. Seeing a few Black faces in high places was important for them to feel that they were part of a successful struggle with tangible results.

Why, then, is there a problem if everyone seems to gain from more integrated workplaces? The problem is the same as having a baseball game and all the players are pitchers or having a football game and each team fielded eleven quarterbacks. The development of the Black community requires *a sense of balance and role playing* like any other situation. If all trained Blacks achieved corporate placement, who would be left to run the Black businesses in our community? Better yet, who in the Black community would be prepared to start and develop the new level of Black enterprises that would require extensive computers, information systems, and an international trade division? Certainly not our newly minted Black MBA's, not the way things are going now. The problem is that the emphasis is virtually totally toward educated Blacks trying to find some White entity to work for just as the uneducated Blacks had worked for White entities millions of times before. The problem is that Black folk have an extremely difficult time comprehending the idea of working for themselves regardless of *how much education they get*. And the *real* problem is that these problems have yet to even be identified in the Black community as problems. As a matter of fact, most of the Black community views as a problem the fact that White firms, corporations and professional associations are still not hiring enough Blacks. They point to the low percentages of partners in law and accounting firms and the lack of representation in upper management in the Fortune 1000 and regret that their battle is still not won. I've heard gifted Blacks say that they were *forced* to set up their own practice because the corporate world would not accept them. In other words, they are saying the Brains of the Black community are not being drained away *fast enough*. Even those who are standing on their own are not doing so willingly but by default. They would rather be where the White action is.

Who is Running Black Business?

It's been stated for the last twenty years that the day of the Mom and Pop stores are over. Today, and certainly the future, we will find most enterprises will be part of some chain, franchise or large corporation. In the Black community in most urban areas that I've seen, Mom and Pop stores are still growing strong. There is a major difference however—the Mom and Pop stores that I see growing in the Black community are Moms and Pops that are not native Americans but who have come from overseas to make a go of what they have said won't work anymore.

If the Mom and Pop stores are being run by non-Blacks in the Black community, and if national franchises and chain stores, owned usually by Whites or others, are growing in the Black community, where are the *Black* businesses in our community? If the people who are most aware of business practice are being hired out of the community, who is running Black businesses? These questions are the key questions that I think need to be raised to understand why Black businesses are the way they are. If one asks the right questions, the answers sometimes are self-evident.

Today's Black businesses are being run by several kinds of personalities with different backgrounds and motivations. A substantial number of businesses are still being run by Mom and Pop. These older businesses are located not in the malls or shopping centers but along the old commercial strips commonly referred to as the "main drag."

These businesses have been basically the same for years; everything in the store is pretty much located exactly where it has always been located for twenty years. When these owners pass on, it is very likely that the business will die, rather than be sold or taken over by their children.

Another group of Black businesses are being run by younger people who have neither training in the more established rules of business or an understanding of the many tools and services of today's business culture. But they are willing to learn and take risks, so they fly by the seat of their pants (skirts) and wing it. Because they are willing to hustle, they make up for a large portion of the mistakes they make. They survive like many of us because they do what they know they have to do to survive. As much as we've been programmed to believe in institutionalized education, you never really know if you are on target except by trial and error anyway. By keeping a tight control on their operational and personal budgets, it is not at all surprising that many, perhaps most, business success stories come from this wide-ranging group.

The other broad group of people who are running a few of the businesses owned by Blacks (but maybe not in the Black community itself) are the new Black entrepreneurs. The new Black entrepreneurs almost always are college graduates and have significant work experience, savings, credit and skills. Many have political contacts or are in situations where they have special access to the very kinds of things that Blacks traditionally have not had access to. These new entrepreneurs are opening up franchises, buying existing successful businesses and are the prototype of what the community needs in the years to come. Unfortunately, like most good things, they are few and far between.

Corporate Junkie vs. The New Black Entrepreneur

We have examined in substantial depth many reasons to explain why Black businesses are as underdeveloped as they are. Among the reasons mentioned was the idea of the Black Brain Drain which I think is a factual reality that no person can deny. But it is also important that we understand that the Black corporate employee is also in significant instances a victim of circumstances which probably most people would fall prey to if they were in a similar set of circumstances. I would like to summarize my analysis of how the community is being drained of its brainy potential business leaders and how in many instances the Black corporate employee is an unwilling or at least a frustrated participant in the process.

To begin with, I think many Black students enter college with an intention to improve the general conditions for their people in some way, in addition to striving for their personal advancement. Business students have very often been heard to say something like, "Well, when I get out of school, I'm going to work for "the man" for a few years and then take my savings and open my own business in the community." I believe everyone reading this book has heard statements similar to this and there is a pretty good chance that you have said it yourself.

When the students leave school with their business, engineering, computer and law degrees, they apply to and are often accepted by the government or corporate sectors. They are twenty-two or so years old and they have the desires of a twenty-two to twenty-five year old. You don't think about sacrifice after you've eaten peanut butter and jelly sandwiches to get through college.

So, our young graduate gets the car, the apartment, the stereo system, the video system, the clothes, the credit cards, the basic apartment furnishings and soon they are in serious debt. Also, the school loans are now due to be paid now that graduation is over and that represents several thousand dollars of additional debt. By twenty-seven or twenty-eight years old, the majority of these students will be married or have children to support or both. By the time the children and/or marriage comes, the company benefit package takes a new position of importance. Previously, you may have been in perfect health but the prudent person with responsibilities now cares about medical coverage, life insurance, a dental plan perhaps, the pension plan and all the things that one would hate to have to pay out of one's own earnings. Very quickly, these benefits are taken for granted.

Five or so years into the company and you've been on more planes, seen more cities, dined in more fine hotels and enjoyed more ego boosting experiences than your mother, your father and your grandmother have ever experienced in their lives put together. In another year or so, you will be eligible for a profit sharing plan where you will own company stock and, of course, you are either in your own home or moving out of your starter home and into a place and a neighborhood you are really proud of. At least one child (by your first or second spouse) is also near school age. So here you are, thirty-two to thirty-five years old and much more in need of the steady and sure income from that corporate job than you have ever been before, You are *hooked, a corporate junkie, in that you cannot live without it*. You may complain about the racism, the lack of promotional opportunities, the petty politics, the boring company functions, the phony personalities and smiles of the people you see every day, but you ain't goin' nooo where,—NOWHERE.

This then is just another part of why Black businesses are the way

they are. The potential business leaders and developers who started out
with all the right intentions, got themselves in a position (based on life's
normal twists and turns), where they either can't leave, are scared to leave,
or think it would be foolish to leave. The bottom line is . . . they stay
in the corporate structure.

The new Black entrepreneur is a rare bird. Someway, he or she has
kept their eye on the goal all the time. They enjoyed all the trips, the meals,
the awards and promotions, but they have a *need* to run their own thing.
That need surpasses anything that the corporation can offer. Every day
they ask themselves, "what if I could do this (whatever function they've
mastered for the corporation) for my own business? Most people in my
community don't know this stuff even exists." The new Black entrepreneur
is dominated by the need to realize their potential and to chase their vision of what they are absolutely convinced that they can build, develop
or achieve. They are dominated by the idea of having *impact*, not being
just another piece in a 3,000 piece machine (the corporation) that would
not even miss them if they were to disappear. The new Black entrepreneur
absolutely refuses to respect some of the simple-minded supervisors whom
he or she is supposed to follow, and they are sick and tired of reading
about people with less experience than themselves find success in the real
world. The new Black entrepreneur must plan to leave because it will only
be a matter of time before they will be pushed to the point of abruptly
quitting or being fired. This is the mentality of this bold, new breed of
Black talent, but they are rare—simply because guts and ambition are rare.

Unfortunately for the new Black entrepreneur, they are very often
misunderstood and even disliked. Their White associates think they're up-
pity and their Black ones think them egotistical ("You ain't no different
from the rest of us, Fred; why can't you just be cool and go along with
the program like the rest of us. It's only a game.") It's very important
that Black people understand that White folks go through this same thing
also, especially White women. America has always called itself the home
of the free and the brave but most Americans, White and Black alike, have
been jealous and puzzled by anyone who dared to be *brave* and be *free*.

In my last publication, I stated that fortune builders share common
traits. Among those traits is the idea that they have either a supportive
spouse or no spouse at all. I would like to describe what has happened
and what will unfortunately continue to happen when Black men and women
try to break away and start their own business.

A Man's Conflict With His Wife

A man does not get a chance to give birth to a baby. It is very, very important for a woman to understand that. A man may father a child, assist in the birth of that child, help feed, clothe and teach that child, but that is not the same as actually giving birth. If you listen real close to a man talk about his business, it sounds very much like he is talking about his child and, in a very real way, he is. Because starting, "nursing," and building a business is about as close as a man will ever get to childbirth. Once a man has decided to start a business (get pregnant—expecting to deliver a beautiful creation), it can easily start the dissolving of a marriage if the wife doesn't go along. Why wouldn't a wife go along with her Black husband starting his own business? Let me count the ways.

1. **Fear of risk**: All businesses are risky and Black businesses are even more so. Statistics and personal observation says the chances are much greater that it will fail than that it will succeed. The cold-blooded truth is that this is the cold-blooded truth.

2. **Why give up a sure thing?**: The potential business owner has a good salary, good benefits and "security." Why give that up to take a chance on something that might happen but probably won't happen.

3. **Wasted talent, time and effort**: If our Black man is an engineer and has a business idea that does not involve engineering, his wife, family, friends and community will often feel that *we* (Black People) *are losing* an engineer. "What a waste of talent," they say. "He's throwing away his career, his mother's heart is broken because of her sacrifices, etc." It's a real shame that Black Folk get so hung up in images and status. The Black community never had an engineer in the first place. General Motors or IBM or Polaroid had the engineer. *He was theirs* and *they paid for him* and *all the enginering he ever did was for them*. The Black community no more "lost" an engineer than they "lost" the Viet Nam War. Our Black entrepreneur candidate, however, can fall for the gobbley-gook, withdraw his dreams and remain with the master.

4. **A fall in our lifestyle**: It takes years in the normal course of events to get one's life on track economically, professionally, maritally, etc. A wife can very easily ask "why, when we have gone through so

much struggle to get where we are, do you decide at *this time* to go through a whole set of *new changes* and sacrifices to land who knows where ten years later. Is this fair to the family?" (This question can instill a great deal of guilt.)

5. **Loss of status**: Let me ask a question of Black women. If you could marry a corporate executive making 65 thousand dollars a year or a McDonald's owner making a hundred and five thousand dollars a year, which one would you marry if they were identically attractive twins? Women's lib is here to stay and I support most of its principles . . . but old ways die hard.

Women, and I can't honestly say Black women more than White, live through their men. The status that the man develops in the job is like a beam of light that shines over the whole family. There are many social affairs, pictures in the newspaper, presents, awards, and trips that come to the wife of a successful man because of his position. The status of a woman among her own friends many times is flushed down the toilet if she and her husband break up. So for that reason, wives may beg their husbands to stay in the corporate world, because even though she doesn't work there, it has been "her" world also. She stands to lose her position in life if he walks away from his.

If a "friend" who knows your husband was a corporate lawyer with an impressive reputation (and a beautiful thirty-fourth floor overlooking-the-bay-office) walks up to you and says, "I heard he's making hamburgers now," would you as a wife feel embarrassed at *your loss of status* or would you feel that your dumb friend has yet to learn that it's independence and money that bring contentment to people? Many women would be embarrassed.

6. **This is your dream . . . not mine**: When a couple work in separate companies, they carry their own weight to earn the salaries they receive. The man seldom performs the wife's jobs and vice versa. But, in a business, one person usually has the big dream, the other partner is often a reluctant participant. Some women have no problem in their husband going into business except if it is an automatic assumption that she too is to dive in with as much work, and hope and expectation as he. Something good can be said for "separate but equal."

The Woman's Conflict With Her Husband

The woman's desire to go into business can be stifled for some of the same reasons that a woman would stifle a man's. There is concern about giving up a sure thing for this "business kick you're on right now." The man might be concerned about the debt that he too will be responsible for as they sign the note for the second mortgage loan, etc. But usually there is not much concern with a fall in status; he is who he is, irrespective of his wife's employment.

The man's concern, is much more directed to his ego. Whereas the woman might fear business because of a belief in her man's *failure* to make it go, a man's concern seems to most often involve his belief that his wife *will be successful* and how that success is to affect their relationship.

1. **Well, what about the children and the house**: In virtually every culture in the world, the female takes care of the young. Of course, there is no gene in women marked BABYSITTER or HOUSEWIFE but traditions die hard. Basically, a woman needs to show what alternatives exist, the cost of the alternatives and the benefits to be derived if your business is a success. Men and Women have to *sell* their spouses on the business before they meet any bankers or customers. The normal routine that was established prior to the business idea as well as the ages and needs of the children will help decide this very common concern.

What men experience in pondering their wives going into business is not objections as such, but fears. Fears not of failure but fears of success.

2. **What if she starts to make more money than me?**: Manhood has historically been equated with control and was dictated to a cetain extent by who controlled the purse strings. Obviously, if a woman starts to make more money, men feel less in control and thus often less of a man.

3. **What if she starts to find me dull and boring?**: Depending on the kind of business one is in, of course, business progress is often decided by *deals*. Deals with people in town, across the state, on the West Coast, etc. When you deal on a national or regional or even statewide basis, it can become hard to get excited about what happened in

somebody's office that day. If that's all that that person can talk about (as you unpack from your week-end business trip) that can indeed get to be boring, even if you don't want it to be.

4. **What if she meets somebody more interesting, attractive, sexy, powerful, etc., than me?**: Obviously things are relative. If one's travels and dealings with people on a business level are broader than they were when you were an employee, you will meet more people and you will meet them from a different vantage point. Instead of representing someone else, you will represent yourself, *your business*. Instead of just talking, you will be negotiating, which is a different kind of talking. It is quite possible that in a particular town after a particularly good dinner at a particular restaurant, you might find a particular man more appealing than your husband. At least for that particular moment (that night). It's not that a husband is making this up; he knows how those things can go because perhaps he has experienced them himself.

5. **What if she gains more status, fame or success than me?**: In this day and age, when people who sell a lot of cookies, or chickens or donuts or anything, can get their picture in papers, magazines or on television, it is quite possible that a successful female-run enterprise can get the headlines. Indeed, if a Black woman does one day what White males do every day, it *is* news. Women have their own magazines and therefore a successful Black business woman's story can theoretically be of interest to women all across the nation. In a male-dominated society, it is easy for a man to feel slighted if he lives in the shadow of a better known or more successful wife. Of course, it may not be right or fair, but I think it is true.

What I am trying to say here are several things at once. I'm saying that in spite of the best of intentions, plans and goals, many Black folks who plan to set up businesses in our community do not do so because the natural or usual flow of events causes them to cling to their 9–5 jobs. Some, in fact, become addicted to all the perks and goodies that corporations have to give. I am saying also that both men and women who do in fact manage to develop the determination to start their own business have to struggle with their spouses for an assortment of concerns and reasons before they realize their dream. Sometimes, spouses have to select between their marriage and their business and people act on both sides of this issue. I'm saying also that the Black community loses virtually every time the new Black entrepreneur fails to exercise their dream. And I'm saying that the concern with wives involves her assumptions that her husband will fail while a husband's concern involves his assumption that his wife will be a success. And, finally, I'm saying that this is not only why Black businesses are the way they are but why they are likely to continue to be underdeveloped for some time to come.

Why Black Business Are The Way They Are- Summary

I could easily list other reasons to explain why our businesses are the way they are but I think all of the basic points are here. Therefore, I will review them in order that the points and perspective can be drawn together:

1. Black people are saturated with about a dozen attitudes which lead our people to have a definite anti-money and anti-wealth perspective. These attitudes evolved from and were nurtured by our history, culture, institutions, and our position as victims in American society. In spite of this, however, we have a lot of pride and admiration for those rich Blacks among us that society has designated "stars." We allow and condone behavior and values from these "stars" that we do not tolerate from any other members in the community. These attitudes act as a strong deterrent from starting businesses for the prupose of making large amounts of money.

2. In those instances when Blacks do start their own business, the prime motivation is very often not money but for reasons which strictly please the emotions or ego of the business owner. And in those instances, when there is the initial goal of starting a business for the purpose of making money, the owner almost inevitably settles for a sum very near what they were making as a salaried employee.

3. Black businesses do not get the complete patronage of Black people because Blacks have as consumers developed a set of standards and expectations which they have grown accustomed to and demand of all businesses. Many black businesses have not grown as fast in catering

to customers' wants as the customers have moved to developing their wants. Many Black business owners are still of the opinion that their businesses should be patronized for the primary reason that they are a Black business. The issue is strongly divided in our community with ample justification on both sides.

4. A chief reason contributing to the continued underdevelopment of Black businesses lies in the fact that counter to a historical trend of Black leaders and thinkers serving the community, today's Black thinkers largely serve the interests of corporate America. This has been called the "Black Brain Drain" and would be an even greater problem in our community if corporations opened their doors even further for the skilled and talented Blacks ready and extremely willing to take corporate positions.

5. Today's Black businesses are being run by older Mom and Pop operators and young people largely using a trial and error method and from whom emerge many of our moderately successful businesses. There are a few Black businesses being run by former corporate employees whose drive to set up their own shop is stronger than those of the associates that he or she left behind in the corporate world. These Black business-people are part of the wave of the future and though they operate some of the most sophisticated Black-owned businesses, they are still rather few in number.

6. Inside the major White corporations one finds two basic types of Black employees. The first type of employee is that one which started out with the intention to eventually leave the corporate world at some time in the future to establish a Black enterprise. However, due to the personal debts, commitments, responsibilities, and advice that this employee obtains over time, they elect to stay in their job situation. Some change to the degree that they become like "junkies," unable to imagine how they could exist outside of the corporation and all its goodies. The second type of Black employee is that one which has never lost sight of their desire and need to start their own enterprise. Unfortunately, if this person overcomes all the usual and expected problems and hassles of starting a business, they may find that their biggest obstacle is to convince a spouse who for a host of reasons may have a problem with their partner having their own business. Some spouses

are pushed into a corner where they are just about forced to choose between their business aspirations and their spouse, and they make the decision according to the strength of their conviction.

7. All the conditions listed here account for a significant amount of the underdevelopment of Black business; but, even worse, there are no significant clues that substantial changes are in the process of happening, which gives the indication that most Black businesses will remain the way they are.

MAKING THE TRANSITION FROM EMPLOYEE TO BUSINESS OWNER

Black Folks Guide To Business Success has as its purpose the delivery of information to its readers which will help them run successful businesses. We feel that a great number of lessons can be learned by understanding what *not* to do as well as what to do. Black businesses have more often been examples of what not to do, which is why we have taken so much effort to dissect them and examine them. We believe that every time a person learns how to eliminate a habit or attitude that has led to the downfall of thousands of other businesses (White as well as Black) we feel that you are increasing your chances of survival. Obviously, one must survive before one prospers, just as surely as one must crawl before one walks.

In spite of all the negative reporting in the previous pages with respect to our past and present conditions, there was a positive intention in it all. Running a business can be something like walking through a mine field. We are merely trying to tell you where the mines are so that you can avoid them.

I feel very confident that we are beginning an explosive new era of Black business ownership. These businesses will be of unprecedented quality. They will be successful not only by eliminating the attitudes and habits listed in the previous chapters, but, in some cases, by adopting the very opposite attitudes and habits which have handicapped us thus far. All people's traditions (including Black folks) must change to adapt to new facts and information. Yesterday's delicious soul food is today's high salt, high cholesterol diet that causes hypertension and a host of other ailments. We must change or we will continue to suffer; it's that simple. Today's young Black businesspeople do not have an overly romantic or exaggerted notion of our past traditions. People today want to know *what will work, period!* Black businesses also will prosper because we will not be dependent on some outside white authority to pick and choose who tomorrow's Black leaders will be. Unlike college admissions, corporate positions, military or government jobs where a committee or director selects the "Proper Neegrow" for the role model positions, business leaders select themselves. Business owners decide themselves to go into business and decide how much business they are going to do. Of course, only a small percentage of business owners of any race really reach their business goals. The point is, however, that no specific person or committee can tell a person that they can't become a successful businessperson, and no specific person is singled out and excluded from participating in the process. This cannot be said about law, medicine, dentistry, etc. We assume that our readers are already interested in starting their own businesses and also are very clear that Black businesses have to meet virtually the same quality, quantity and service standards of any other American business. We want to shed some light on how to get *from here to there*. How do you prepare for the changes and demands of being your own boss when you are currently employed somewhere else? Virtually everything that you have read on that topic so far has probably focused on financing, marketing, finding a location to work from, developing a business plan and all the other basic aspects of starting a business. All of these functions are indeed important and fortunately this type of information is available everywhere.

What is not available is the different mind-set, personality and perspective the business person must adopt to generate the type of success that they are fully capable of. We are going to discuss that under-developed topic, the personal dimensions of getting from here to there. What typical reactions can you expect from family, friends and neighbors as you begin to run your own show? How can you tell if what you are losing is more important that what you are gaining, or vice versa? And most importantly, how does one prioritize the many tasks and not get lost in the woods among the many trees? We know that if a person loses their sense of what they are doing or why they are doing it during the early years of turmoil in business, they may very well quit before their enterprise had had a chance to blossom. As was mentioned before, developing a business is like (I imagine, since I've never done it myself) giving birth to a child. You are not sure the sickness, the fat, the sacrifices and the physical pain are worth it until it's all over, when you deliver and see what you have created.

How Much Does It Cost?

The central question that lies under virtually every aspect of the turmoil associated with business is a question of cost. When one knows the cost of something ahead of time, one can make sound judgments. But when we get halfway into any situation and find out at that point that the true cost is higher than we expected, it is easy and natural to become angry, frustrated, discouraged and nonfunctional. In an effort to demonstrate our point, we are going to relate a story about Janice.

Janice, a female executive, walked into a fashionable store one day and saw a beautiful coat which she immediately adored. She pulled it from the rack and held it out at arm's length. Yes, she thought, it was truly stunning. Her free hand worked its way down to the sleeve so she could find the price tag. She closed her eyes momentarily as if she was making a wish that the price wouldn't blow her right out of the front door. She found the tag and flipped it over. She noticed the nine right away, but the zeroes behind it all seemed to run together. She strained her eyes a second to find the decimal point. She found it after the third zero. Wow, she thought, nine thousand dollars. Well, she thought, it was no bargain but it could have been higher. Her powers of rationalization sharpened quickly and her mind was now flying at a mind-boggling pace. Janice went down the rack and peeped at every other fur and its price. A few were priced higher but most were lower. None of the coats struck her as being as attractive as the one she was considering purchasing. She went back to her first choice and the wheels in her head kept turning. After trying the coat on, she concluded that the coat's price was definitely not a rip-off, but whether she could afford it was another question. Janice left the store but continued to ponder that absolutely incredible fur that she had seen. She was a smart cookie, a plotter and a planner since high school, and a good money manager as well. The last eighteen months had been stressful but very profitable. She was leaning toward rewarding herself. The central question she had to ask herself was, how much was this flawless coat really going to cost? She knew that the price tag said nine thousand, *so that was a hint of the cost*. Janice makes fifty-three thousand dollars a year before taxes. That would mean that the coat would cost almost *three months of sixty-hour workweeks* in after-tax money. If Janice puts part of her eight thousand dollar savings on the coat, it will cost her the *security* she now feels with that bankroll. If she uses her credit card to pay for the coat, she's likely to pay about fifty dollars a month *in interest* for the next couple of years, boosting the real cost of the coat above ten thousand dollars. If she buys the coat, she will not be in a position to buy any other fashions for at least the *next eighteen months*. If she buys the coat, then *the trips to South America and Europe*, trips she had been planning for over a year, would be completely postponed for at least another two years. If she bought the coat, there would be all the snide remarks from her family and friends, brought on by jealousy, envy or frustration. She doesn't want to have to hear all that junk, and, besides, they probably would start asking for more loans than they do right now. Janice also must ask herself, "If I buy the coat, *what will I wear with it?*" She likes her current wardrobe, but nothing seems elegant enough to wear with a nine thousand dollar coat. Also, *where would she wear* the coat? If she isn't going on her vacations and she continues her sixty-hour work weeks, there would be minimum opportunities for her to strut her stuff in this coat. If she were to only wear the coat, say 10-12 times over the next two years or so, that would be like charging yourself *a thousand dollars a night* to wear a coat. Janice is still single and she also wonders if such an expensive coat would *attract or intimidate* the man of her dreams. Only when Janice has added up all the consequences, ramifications, sacrifices and costs of this appealing coat will she have a picture of the *true cost of the coat*. It will cost not just ten thousand dollars (taxes and interest). It will cost a bit of her feeling of security, cancelled vacations and a greatly reduced allowance for other clothes, all for the privilege of wearing it only a few times a year with other garments she is not comfortable with, while drawing uncertain responses from the people around her. Whatever her decision, she will be in a much better position to make it after tallying up the pluses and minuses. The price tag alone is not nearly enough.

Do people actually ask themselves these many questions before a major purchase? Probably very few do. Most people look at the monthly payment and determine if they can afford it. But everyone (except the rich, of course) experiences the consequences and problems of having made expensive, un-thought-out purchases. I know people who could not qualify to purchase a house that was within their grasp simply because they had bought a new car about a year before and had three years of hefty payment still to make on it. The point is, major commitments—such as expensive purchases, marriage, children, divorce, partnerships, and business ownership—need detailed study because you will *almost always* pay more than you had planned. The "price tag price" is just the beginning. Ask Janice.

Paying the Cost to Be the Boss

Do most people take themselves through the third degree before starting a business? The answer is no, they don't. Many people feel if they ask themselves too many questions they will back out of the effort altogether. The questions people do ask (and rightly so) involve the mechanics or methods of operating their business. They may have a few concerns about the effect of the business on their personal life, but they can handle it, they think; and they pronounce themselves ready to do "bidness." When they actually get into the business, and the true costs, consequences and sacrifices become known, too often, people will pick that time to ask "if it is all worth it." A sudden streak of bad luck, a loss of confidence or an unexpected but modest injury can be just the thing to put a potentially good person and business out of business.

In trying to get you from here to there, we are going to examine the true and total costs of business success. There are going to be some things that we will leave out; that is unavoidable. And, also, it stands to reason that not everyone will pay exactly the same price; some will pay more or less than others. But we feel that since everyone has been telling you to strive for success and "be all that you can be," that somebody ought to be out here telling you how much all this "success" is going to cost. Perhaps if we knew the complete cost, many of us would choose to redefine our definition of success and thereby be happier individuals for doing so.

Don't Expect A Lot of Genuine Support

It takes a person of strong discipline and self-confidence to start and develop a business. Not only must you be willing to live life at the bare bones level and put your money where your mouth is, most of the time you will have to do it without much support from the people who you love and who love you. This section is being written to explain what happens and why it happens to many amibitious business owners, especially Black ones.

If you are a goal-oriented person making a good salary in either the corporate, public or government sectors, you undoubtedly have many friends who fit that same category. You and your associates probably read the lastest magazines, keep up with the news and generally study the social, political and business scene. If you do these things it is virtually impossible for you not to be aware of the great increases in the numbers of people of all races who are going into their own business. It is also very likely that many of your associates have discussed going into business themselves. These "entrepreneurial discussions" can be a great source of information and encouragement as you hear friend after friend detail some idea they have, somebody else has or something they've read in a paper or magazine. Entrepreneurship, like so many things in this country, can saturate the media so thoroughly that it becomes a fad, an in-thing to talk about and to aspire to. Young, urban professionals, which includes Blacks as well (Yuppies and Buppies), like to feel that they are "up" on things and by all means would like their associates to believe that they are up on things as well. So it's of no major significance I'm saying, if one hears or participates in many chats about going into business, everybody's doing it. However the reality is that most "Buppies" are corporate or job junkies (discussed previously), and for all the talk you may hear, at least 90% have no plans or intentions of going anywhere but perhaps to a "better" job in the foreseeable future. It's not that they don't believe that running your own enterprise is a great accomplishment; on the contrary, they believe it must be a wonderful position to be in. It's just that they don't ever really see themselves as having their act and their heart so together that they would quit their job and go on their own. Virtually everyone in the lunch group or bar group (or whatever) believes that everyone else in the group is pretty much like themselves—just talking. As long as no one breaks ranks, everything is fine, because every member of the group thinks very highly of themselves—being "first generation college" and first of their family in such a prestigious corporate or government job.

Now, you come along and announce to the group, "Next Friday's my last day. I'm going to start my own business on the first of the month."

What do you think each group member is going to feel? Some will think you're stupid for walking away from such a good job. Some will be jealous of your ability to take a position and go with it. There will be all sorts of reactions from the "gang at work," but virtually all of them will *smile and wish you well.* Most of them will try very hard to separate their own ambitions, situations, and talents from yours, but most will fail to do so. Even though everyone will wish you well on the outside, many, perhaps most, of them will *hope that you fail.* Why? Because your new independence and determination is now the cause of a great sense of unsettling pressure within them. By your making a move, you are forcing them to ask themselves if they should make a move. You are making it more difficult for them to *talk* about doing their own thing, because your movement has now made a difference between action and talk.

When you leave the workplace, you become everyone's guinea-pig. Everybody wants to know how you are "coming along." If reports circulate that you are doing poorly, they will feel badly for you but better about themselves. They will feel that they made the "wise decision" to stay on the job where they have security, seniority, pension, etc. Your failure is proof that business is not as easy as it appears to be when you read about it in those glossy covered magazines. Your friends may indeed draw closer to you because, like a martyr, your failure helped save them from anguishing decisions.

If, however, you succeed, you create tremendous pressure for some of the members of the "old gang at work." Your business success now gives you more money, freedom, attention, contacts, etc. It was just a few years before that you were all "around the table, talking," and you were all on equal footing. Now, you have surpassed them all. What do you think your friends are thinking about *themselves* after they see what you have done? While many may be very contented in their positions and very happy for you, at least a few are wondering at least a little harder what they should do with the rest of their lives. And you "caused" this problem for them with your success. What happens in many cases is that people solve the mystery (the mystery of your success) by saying to themselves and others that you were *lucky.* It is important that luck rather than your ability be the thing which got you over, because for years your former associates had always evaluated your abilities and your intelligence as being no better than their own. Perhaps they even felt you had less ability than themselves. It is difficult for them to now believe that you became smarter or that they became dumber, so, therefore, the answer has to be luck. Most hard-working successful people are driven up the wall when their efforts are denied and their success is attributed to luck. You will probably be no different.

What exactly does all this mean, you might be asking. What I am saying is that it is now time for Black America to rise up in the business world; everybody knows it or says it. However, the brave men and women who step forward and make the decisions and the moves unfortunately cannot depend on their family and friends to support them, because business success says one hell of a lot about what a person is made of and it separates people of real substance from people who just talk and play a role. Business success seems to divide people and cause envy and jealousy almost the way light skin and straight hair did back in the 1950's. The big difference, however, is that skin and hair is a matter of heredity; you either have it or you don't. Business success is a matter of guts, growing, determination, sacrifice and similar characteristics. It is not a matter of either having them or not. It *is* a matter of one's willingness to *pay the price* or not. Most people do not want to pay the price, and they get upset when they see that someone else is. When you go into your own business, don't expect too much support from family and friends. They love you, but they're just scared of the responsibility of being responsible, and the challenge of making something where nothing existed before. Please, please do not let that affect you!

Intellectual Costs

By far, the greatest cost involved in starting a new enterprise is the intellectual cost—meaning being willing to pay the price of learning new things. One of the problems with Blacks is that they have been sold on the supreme power of colleges. Many of us feel that once we have a degree, and certainly a graduate degree, that there are few books that can tell us anything. Business is always changing because there is money to be made in changing for the better. Someone always finds out how to do something better. Someone always finds out how to do something faster or cheaper. One has to be a student of one's industry. Many Blacks can make music, write books, act or repair cars; but unless we become *students* of the record, book, theatre, or automobile *industries*, we will almost always come out on the short end of the stick. By far, the greatest area of intellectual dues we have to pay is that involving sales. Selling is a thinking, not an inborn or automatic or even common sense, activity. Black folks have to learn how to think like salespeople, because without sales they have no business, period. Every hour of every day, *millions of times per hour*, money changes hands in exchange for a good or a service. The people who are receiving the money *in their own behalf* (not sales clerks) are doing the selling. People who sell usually receive money at least five of the seven weekly days. If someone receives money twenty days per month and you, as an employee, only receive money (your pay) twice a month, there is a good chance that the person whose business it is to receive money ten times as often as you *will make more money than you do.*

Selling and marketing and promotion and advertising are all related and merit at least one entire book of study. We are only stating here that this is part of the intellectual cost of going into business. Selling is to business what running is to sports.

In addition to becoming a student of the industry that your business is related to and a student of the art of selling, you have to be a student of your customers—their problems, wants, lifestyles, etc. The people are going to be the ones to give up the money. You must study them. What do they want; why do they want it; how do they want it; when do they want it; how long will they want it; and what will they pay for it? Business people are some of the most remarkable people in the world, not because they went to college or the like, but because they know people so very, very well. Believe me, they weren't born that way.

Financial Costs

The nature of the business one enters will dictate the amount of money one has to put up to start an establishment. The amount of backing, collateral, savings, etc., will dictate one's ability to raise the necessary cash. But the concept of financial cost is not so much measured in dollars and cents as it is in an attitude that business people adopt. That attitude is one of sacrifice and delayed gratification. I find that I have to very often differentiate between sacrifice and poverty. I have heard people say that they have sacrificed because "of all these years going without a decent wardrobe or a decent car or a decent vacation." When I looked at these people's financial situation a bit closer, I found that they weren't sacrificing, they were simply poor. They did not have and never had the money to purchase what they were complaining about. Sacrifice is not poverty. Sacrifice is having the money, being able to go to the bank or pull a credit card to actually buy what you want, but *deciding not to do it* because that money and that time and that credit line can best be used to help the business grow. Financial costs in this context means sacrifice. It means being able to look at a pile of money on the table and put it where the *business* dictates it should go rather than where your *heart or your ego* thinks it should go. That entails some emotional as well as financial costs.

Another part of financial cost involves property ownership. If possible, Blacks should own the site that their business is located on, for several reasons. First, ownership puts control in the business owner's hands. Non-ownership means that a person can be put out of business simply by a landlord deciding to go up on rent. And if they see a prosperous business, believe me, *they will* go up on rent. Secondly, ownership also makes you a better credit risk and credit is very important to a beginning or expanding business. A creditor feels more secure that you will be there for him to collect his money, and he has something to which he can attach a lien if you are buying your facility. Thirdly, when you are ready to sell your business, you are in a better position to get full value when you are selling actual property along with the ongoing enterprise. Financial costs here relate to the responsibility of purchasing and maintaining property.

All businesses have to do a certain amount of advertising and promoting of their products and services. Advertising for a business is like feed for a prized pet. If you stop feeding the pet, it loses its vitality and eventually its life. In business, one can probably get away for a while with little advertising, but eventually you must advertise to grow.

In business, if you are not planning to grow, you will almost certainly shrink. The financial cost of running a business sometimes involves bringing in money from the outside to pump new life into a sagging business, much like artificial respiration acts as an outside source of air to revive an unconscious person. It is much easier to understand business if you understand it to be a living thing that requires almost the very same things that other living things require.

Physical and Time Costs

Many businesses are very demanding physically, and virtually all full-time businesses are demanding of one's time. Physically, many businesses are demanding in that you simply have to stand on your feet for eight to twelve hours a day depending on the type of business and the amount of assistance you have. Some businesses require you to drive or fly many miles.

Flying is certainly easier than driving, but then eighty or a hundred thousand air miles (and the stress and rushing involved with that) can drain one to the same extent, perhaps, as twenty thousand highway miles travelled for business. Late hours without normal sleep is a basic part of many routines of new business owners.

The reason that running a business is so time-consuming is that a typical owner has to play so very many roles if they are interested in a top-notch operation. Owners have to be idea people and come up with the innovative aspects of their business that will make it unique. They have to be planners in that they have to take some of these great ideas and plan from beginning to end how the ideas are to be made a reality. Owners have to be financial planners in that they have to plan how each dollar is going to be spent. All of these tasks require a quiet time when one can sit and think calmly, reviewing what has taken place thus far and how things can be improved. It is very difficult to get these developmental and planning activities done in the middle of the work day when you have operational and management responsibilities. A business person is virtually always in a promotional frame of mind. How can more people learn about what I have to offer? This is an ongoing, never-ending task. All businesspersons have to do paperwork. They must keep in touch by paper or by phone with people they order products from and sell products to. They must collect money owed to them and pay the people they owe. Finally, as if all of this work was not enough, they must study the trends of their industry, do research and find out what their competitors are doing and why. If a business is open six or seven days a week for ten or more hours a day, it should be very easy to see how a person can become rather saturated with their own enterprise.

Family Costs

Because there are but so many hours in anyone's day, something has got to give, and very often the amount and quality of family time suffers in the early days of the development of a business. If children are involved, and they often are, their birthdays, graduations, baseball games, recitals and other activities are no less important to them than other children's. But as a business owner who has to choose between a great holiday sale on the one hand or a great family holiday vacation on the other, the decisions are often harsh on the feelings and expectations of the family. Sexual desire and the preliminary foreplay may be more like torture for a person that's been on their feet for sixteen hours and is dying for rest and sleep. The whole sense of a "balanced" life is going to a hungry entrepreneur, and often the family has to develop a sense of being unbalanced themselves if there is to be some concept of harmony in the household.

The issues which come up time and again in these situations are as follows: Who is the business owner really doing this for? themselves and their ego or the family? How long will this workaholic behavior continue? Why do they work so hard if they are not getting a chance to enjoy it? What am I supposed to do socially, sexually, and recreationally if they are always too busy? The answers to these questions depend on a lot of factors. For example, how involved are the other family members in the business? The greater their involvement, the greater understanding of and identification with the tasks to be accomplished. This seems to be one tremendous advantage of the newly-arrived immigrants when they set up their enterprises, they do not fall into the American two-career family lifestyle. Another factor is the owner's planning to lead him or herself away from handling every aspect of the enterprise. Have they a plan to free themselves up and are they committed to that plan? A major consideration would be the size and scope of the business being developed. If it is designed to have a city-wide impact and deliver six figure profits, then there is some real intent on providing security for the wife and children after the husband's passing, and this should be appreciated. If, however, the profits from the enterprise are almost immediately used to buy toys and luxuries for the owner, then the motivation is a lot more self-centered.

How well was the family prepared as to what to expect when a mother or father decided to go into business. If the business owner did not prepare the family as to what to expect and what the "costs" were, then the owner must assume a very significant part of the weight for a disrupted family life. Preparation in this sense means total preparation, meaning not only relating the decrease in time together, but the financial sacrifices, the reduction of travel and vacations together, etc. These are just some aspects and examples of the family cost of going into business.

Social Costs

The loss of time for socializing is similar to the problems of lost family time. Many times friendships simply fade away because there is not much in the way of common interests anymore. They get tired of hearing about your business and you get bored with them talking about their job. Other conversation may just reveal how little you know about what else is going on in the world. Other times, socializing has a business intent. You find that you are now around people that you may not particularly like or have much in common with. However, the setting may be one that you need to be in in order to meet people who it will be in your interest to know, or to learn information that is provided only in these types of situations. Business conventions replace intimate house parties. Mixed settings become all male or mostly female meetings.

Genuine concern for friends and warm hugs are replaced by respectful greetings, firm "power" handshakes and a concern for one's "body language." Social cost is a family cost because, whereas the family shared in a certain portion of socializing before, your socializing now might be limited to those absolutely "must" business extravaganzas that your family probably couldn't care less about. As a Black person, you will find isolation more often than not because we are still barely present in the very large share of the American business community. The social isolation of being one of the few Blacks at a gathering that is really intended to be a "party" is indeed part of the price you pay for trying to keep up with your enterprise.

Emotional Costs

Because, as was mentioned earlier, the relationship between an owner and their business is somewhat like a parent and child, it should be easy to imagine that the ups and downs of a business can strongly affect the emotional health of the owner. Most Black people struggle in their early years in business, no matter how well prepared they are. Thus, even though business people are optimists by nature (usually), they spend a great deal of time on pins and needles, wondering if they are going to survive. Unexpected problems are rarely matched with unexpected bonanzas. Rather than working the business, the business usually works the owner the first couple of years, and during that period there will inevitably be aspects of your business that you grow to either hate or fear or both. These are two very powerful emotions, and there is no rule to limit how much they can intrude into your enterprise.

Guilt is very easy to experience in business. One can feel guilty that they are not doing the best that they can do. Guilt can come from not spending enough time with friends or family, regardless of your explanations of the demands of the business. Because you have so much control over your own operation, it is very easy to question whether you made the right decisions and if you, in fact, hurt innocent people in making those incorrect decisions. Feelings of insecurity can easily creep up on the most confident of persons in business; all it takes is a run of unexplained problems. The longer one has been used to collecting what seemed like very good wages, the easier it is, I imagine, to wonder if you made the right decision of going into business.

Because people who start their own business have no concrete means of determining their sales and profit margins, they often go by projections of sales. If sales fall significantly below sales projections, it is quite normal to expect our optimistic business owner to experience doubts and disappointment. If a promotional campaign was done with a lot of effort and money, and it did not bring in the customers, there is disappointment and confusion. If the products that are being sold turn out to be less spectacular than you originally envisioned them, then there is disappointment. If the projected sales are, in fact, being made but a bunch of hidden costs eat up a large portion of the profit margin, then there is disappointment. Disappointment is any situation where reality doesn't meet one's expectations, and, because business owners have such high expectations, disappointments are inevitable.

Confusion and uncertainty are other emotions that are part of running an operation. There are so many situations when there is no one to turn to for advice (franchise operations are an exception) that one has to go with their own instincts solely. After what seems like the obvious right decision, there are unexpected or negative consequences. Business people develop a strong stomach for turmoil because it is part of the weekly diet of the active business owner.

If a business owner is not having success balancing their business and family life, but they are, in fact, experiencing business success, it is quite common to feel any empty happiness, or to feel that your efforts and success are not being appreciated. This can be especially true if the success seems to widen the gap between the mates. If there is insecurity or jealousy or envy that did not show its head before, when both spouses were working 9 to 5, those feelings can sometimes come out in the middle of what is supposed to be a period of joyous celebration and destroy a relationship.

The emotion which many Black businesspersons are especially exposed to is the feeling of powerlessness. You begin with what to you seemed like an awful lot of money (your savings, loans from friends, family and banks) and you go into business. Very soon, you discover that your great sum is peanuts in your industry and you see how much abuse you receive and extra expense you have to pay just because you are small and undercapitalized. Of course, the same thing can happen in giant coprorations when a strike idles thousands of workers and millions of dollars are lost in just a few weeks. But the small businessperson is subject to more instances, I think, of situations where the decisions on price, style, inventory, etc., are more or less made for him or her by the decisions of the manufacturers they are dealing with. Federal laws, state laws, local zoning, employment regulations, fire regulations, insurance regulations, IRS regulations, etc., all combine to develop a framework that is so tight that the small business owner finds that many things that they might like to do are completely out of the question.

By far, the greatest emotional cost that a business person is likely to experience, at least in the early stages of their development, is loneliness. When many people start businesses, the only person who really thinks it has a shot at making it is the owner him or herself. Other people may say that the idea sounds good, but then they give you a list of reasons why it probably would not work. Often they are right, and businesses do fail for exactly the reasons they suspected. But just as often people can be wrong, and a determined person can make a way for themselves among the giants. During the testing period, the period between beginning and failing or between beginning and succeeding, it can be the loneliest period of your life. Why? Because as the confident owner, you feel it is important to project a positive attitude regardless of the circumstances, and that means that you don't discuss problems or ask advice from people who may be able to help you. This means that only you know all the problems, the doubts and concerns, and you alone are carrying the weight of those things on your shoulders. This can add to the feeling of aloneness. If a job has to be done, you have to do it or see that it gets done.

We have already mentioned that new owners spend less time with friends and family when they are starting up a business. This isolation, though necessary for the most part, nevertheless adds to the loneliness of the owner. Not only are the spouse and kids missing them, but they are missing the family and the common pleasures of just being around the family. When you are around the family, you really can't feel comfortable with pouring your heart out about the business because that is not what they want to talk about. That may be the last thing they want to talk about. Neither the joy nor the problems can be expected to be understood by the family and friends in the way that they affect you, and in that sense you are alone with your project.

Sometimes the demand and pressures of business success is so encompassing that a person lacks personal time for themselves. Their money, their concerns and time are given to the business, the family and household duties and responsibilities, leaving very little quiet time for one to go over their agenda and priorities. People have a hard time understanding what happens to a person who has not had enough time to sit and think to themselves. Often people assume that because you were away from *them* you are *giving yourself* this valuable time. Now that you are home, you automatically are to switch your total attention to the family that has not seen you for days. People in business really need a hideaway, a place that is not the business, with its one million tasks to be done staring you in the face, nor a place that is home, where you are expected to make up for the lost time. This type of loneliness is yet another cost that the potential business owner should prepare for.

The other side of the loneliness picture is that you will likely be meeting new people every week, perhaps every day. They may be just a smile without a name. Eventually, some of your customers may become true friends. At that point, the payoff of business ownership starts to exceed the mere number of dollars collected in the cash register.

Value Costs

It is difficult to imagine anything that would change one's view of life, one's orientation toward what makes the world go around more than a whole switch from being an employee to a business owner and employer. Your values change dramatically over a period of time. I think that Black people have a fear of developing their perspective. I've heard many people say that if you begin to understand the White man's point of view too well, you become a White man yourself. There is not a single person reading this book who does not know at least half a dozen Blacks who "appear" to fall into this category. But let us substitute some words here so that perhaps another perspective can be developed. If we substitute the words "People in Power" for "White" perhaps we can be a little more objective. To be in power is not a situation to hate; it is a position to strive for and to understand. If Black people's condition is to improve in this country, it will be when we have more power over own lives. Part of the process of getting more power over your life is to understand the perspective and responsibility of people who have power over their lives. It's like anything else, if you want to learn basketball you study basketball players; if you want to study cooking, you watch cooks. It doesn't mean that you have to do what they do just because they do it. But would help you decide what *you* are going to do if you understand *why* they do it the way they do.

Black people out of power, do not like the lifestyle that we are, in many ways, forced to live *because* we are out of power. But if we had a better understanding of power and how to use it, it would help us understand our situation better and help us get power quicker. How do I know this you ask? It's very simple. Even though the world has been plagued with thousands of wars over thousands of years, *most* changes that develop in the world *do not* come about through war. Most changes come about through negotiation. Even the end of war comes about through negotiation. You can only negotiate when you have an idea of what the other party wants without giving up too much of what you want. And you can only have an idea of what the other party wants when you understand their perspective. Thus, Black involvement in business helps us to understand White folks better because a large part of what they are about is business. You usually hate or fear a thing less as you understand it. Thus, Black business people appear perhaps to like White folks easier than nonbusiness owners simply because they understand them better and fear them less.

So, one of the first values to change in business is your fuzzy interpretation on Whites. I do not consider this a *cost* as I have the other categories. I consider this growth and development. The cost is in taking the time and intelligence to try to grow rather than holding onto the popular views of the masses.

The meaning of the word "security" takes on a different value to a businessperson. To an employee, security means degrees, resumés, recommendations, contracts or other so-called guarantees to employment. To a businessperson, there is security in having dealt with many people over the issues of money, goods and services, and in knowing that by merely opening their mouth they can get a total stranger to reach for their wallet and give them their money. When you know that there is virtuallly no city in the nation that someone can put you where you can't use your head, eyes, hands and mouth to get a person to reach for their checkbook, credit card or wallet to give you money for whatever you are selling, *that is security*. Only business people ever know what kind of security that is.

The number of changes in values and perspectives that one goes through are too numerous to mention. Individual differences will vary depending on the nature and location of the business and its clientele. The major point is that business owners will change their interpretation of the world as they better understand the world of business. I believe it is inevitable and desirable. This is not to say that it isn't also desirable for all Black businesspeople to have a sound foundation on their own history and culture. But knowledge of one area of information should not prevent one from understanding and appreciating another area of information. Your personal and business interests are better served with a broader view of your total environment.

Summary

All success has a cost and business success is no different. Although people have their own definition of success, it usually includes having a very substantial salary from their enterprise, having some form of community impact (including the providing of jobs), being a role model for one's children and others in the community and having a deep sense of pride for delivering a quality product or service for which they are known. Typically, the new businessperson understands that the price for this success is defined in terms of sacrifice, money and hard work. They are prepared to give these qualities to reach their goal. What many people are not knowledgeable of and fall prey to are the other costs that go along with business success. These costs relate to their family, friends and their personal emotions and values. It is often these things which cause personal crises to arise rather than the day to day operations of a business. It is important that people who go into business understand completely and quickly what these other costs are in order that they can think about and prepare for them. Not all people will run into all problems. Some even may not experience many of these problems at all. The greatest key to making the transition from employee to business owner is to understand and accept the fact that they are very different roles and require a different mind set. Do not pretend to be the same person as you go through the business development process. You probably will not be successful in business if you insist on holding on to the same ways of thinking as the "gang on the job." Certainly, one need not develop any arrogance toward others, but, after a while, your newly developed confidence will show through and your friends will notice it regardless of how you see yourself.

The most crucial link to your happiness may be your immediate family. There are plenty of successful business people who are miserable because their family came apart during the building of the business. Be very, very clear that it is the business owner's job and their job only to prepare the spouse and children as to what to expect *before* it actually happens. It is also your task to make very clear why all the sacrifices will be worth the struggle. Having done that, all that can be done afterwards is to hope like hell for the best.

A FEW SUGGESTED
BUSINESSES

As a person who travels constantly across the country speaking to various groups about the importance of new financial attitudes and business development for the Black community, I am often asked to name specific businesses that Black folk should enter. I feel it is very unwise to try to answer that question for an individual if you do not know anything about that person's abilities, interests, finances, experience, credit, contacts or the place where they intend to do business.

On the other hand, audiences have a need to be given concrete answers rather than general principles. Some believe that if a published business author cannot give specific examples, well, maybe that author doesn't really know his stuff as well as he should. I have decided, therefore, to include in this work comments about specific businesses. I have no way of knowing if the reader has the capacity for getting involved in these enterprises, but most are not capital-intensive and do not require extensive formal education or extensive licensing. Some, of course, do. What I will try to do is explain why I think these are good businss opportunities and why they might be of particular interest to Blacks. Where possible, I try to mention possible profit margins, but the scale of business is something that individual owners will determine over time. What might be more important to many readers is not the specific businesses that are mentioned but the way in which they are analyzed. I try to make a connection between a commonly-existing Black condition or problem and the business service in response to that condition. Perhaps that same technique can be used to help you analyze your business.

#1. Real Estate Sales

Every year, over a million new residences are built and perhaps about four million residences change ownership. Black people need to get much more involved in the transacton of these properties in order to increase our stake in property ownership. Currently, the education system in public schools and colleges have no means of teaching young people how to buy property or the significance of ownership. This role is not assumed by any institution in our community—the church, unions, fraternities and sororities, social clubs, etc. What that means then is that the only way that young people have to find out about property ownership is through family and friends (if they happen to own property) or through a real estate salesperson looking to do business. It is the real estate salesperson who actually knows the latest information and requirements for property ownership. They are the crucial link between the general public and the owners and financers of property. If the Black community is not adequately represented in this field, the whole race is bound to suffer. Property values are very subjective at times, and since the payment of one's residence is usually the largest single debt and monthly expense, it is quite easy for mistakes to be costly.

The ambitious Black real estate salesperson will not wait for people to come through the office door but will offer their services as a teacher and speak to groups and youngsters on how to buy property and why. After a name is developed as a good teacher, it would stand to reason that the telephones would light up and sales and profits would be made. The market is absolutely flooded with books on real estate in the areas of both sales and investment, so there is no need whatsoever for one to be in the dark about purchasing property.

There are several other reasons why Blacks should look into the real estate field in addition to helping individuals learn about and purchase homes.

First, there should be a strong effort to educate the consumer that virtually all stable communities are those where the residents own the properties rather than temporarily rent them. Ownership generates stronger concern for the quality of the school systems, the quality of municipal services (trash pick-up, street cleaning, etc.) and the quality of elected political representation. If Black residential areas are to improve, ownership will probably be the single strongest link to that improvement.

Secondly, real estate salespeople are no longer confined to restricting their clients to one area or section of town. As long as the industry remains totally run by Whites, it will take much longer for Black people to live in any areas where their money can buy. With the presence of Black salespeople, Black ownership can expand far beyond the ghetto territories that have been for so many years.

The third reason that Black involvement in real estate sales is important is that many businesses are sold through real estate offices because the business includes the sale of real property. Thus, the presence of more Black real estate salespeople will not only make for more ownership of homes but could impact greatly on the number of businsses owned by Blacks also. Rather than waking up one day and finding that your new corner store is owned by a different outsider, you could be alerted to the fact that it was for sale in time enough to own it yourself.

The last reason that we are going to mention in discussing the importance of real estate involves the opportunity for the training of young people in an important and profitable career. The old apprenticeship method of teaching young people under the watchful eyes and encouragement of a master is gone from most vocations today. People are crammed forty to the room, lectured to for two hours and told to go home and read. Sometimes it works and sometimes it doesn't. In real estate, an ordinary person with a high school diploma can enter an office and, in the time it takes to earn a four-year degree, that person can emerge as a competent professional earning a handsome income and dealing successfully with lawyers, bankers, federal agencies and town zoning boards. This is possible because the old student-teacher, master-apprentice relationshp still has a vitality in the real estate industry.

Minimum Requirements: To enter the real estate field one needs a license in virtually every state in the union. Licenses are usually issued after taking a real estate course lasting about 45–60 hours of classroom time and passing a state exam. Real Estate Brokers must pass an additional exam and have two years minimum experience in negotiating a broad range of types of property sales.

Financial Investment Necessary: Salespeople's costs usually involve merely tuition for the course and state exam and license fees. Total

amount should be less than three hundred dollars. Business cards and forms after placement may total another hundred dollars.

Real estate brokers opening their own office may need as much as thirty thousand dollars in order to fully equip themselves with telephones, computers, copy machines, furniture, professional directories, membership dues, etc. This sum is significantly influenced by office location, number of immediate salespeople and local requirements.

Financial Possibilities: Experienced (three years) real estate salespeople make anywhere from fifteen to forty thousand dollars a year, depending upon many factors, including the interest rates, amount of hours put into the job and whether they sell properties other than single family homes. Brokers' incomes are determined by how many active salespeople they have working in their office, their own ability to sell larger projects and their general cost effective management of their offices. Incomes of more than a hundred thousand dollars a year are possible but very rare among Black real estate brokers. Most real estate salespeople eventually look to buy some type of investment property for themselves.

For Further Information: Go to any major bookstore and look through books in the business section. New real estate books come out every week or so. In the library, look in the section of books that begins with the numbers 331 under the Dewey Decimal System.

#2. Apartment Management Specialists

Most Blacks live in urban areas, and in these urban areas we live in three basic places. We live in single-family neighborhoods where individual owners control and manage their own homes. We live in public housing projects where the federal or local government owns, controls and manages the property. And we live in apartment houses where private third-party owners own, control and have management responsibility for the property.

It is quite common in the nineteen-eighties to see something that was a rather rare sight in the nineteen-fifties and -sixties, totally boarded up and abandoned apartment houses. There have been books and reports by the hundreds on why this situation exists and we will not explore it here in any depth. What we will say, however, are several things that explain why this situation is a business opportunity.

First, many, if not most, of these vacant apartment buildings are located in the Black community; therefore, it was Black families—many with young children—that were uprooted and forced to move by the declining buildings. This is not a positive factor in our people's development.

Secondly, the now vacant building invites problems from transients, vandals and drug addicts. Every kind of crime has been committed in vacant buildings, and their frequency of catching (or being set) on fire is notorious.

Thirdly, these vacant buildings detract from the real dollar value of the properties within a several block radius of these buildings. The people who own property near vacant buildings are much slower to invest their money to improve their own property when they see the spread of blight.

Fourthly, a property off the tax rolls just adds to the burdens of those who remain, and people end up paying more money to live in a less desirable place. All of these factors clearly show that it is in no one's interest to see buildings become vacant. Yet, more are becoming vacant every week, and especially in the neighborhoods where the masses of our people live.

The financial opportunity that lies here is that of apartment management. An apartment manager has several roles to play and, although there is a general pattern, specific duties are hammered out between manager and owner. Generally, a building manager interviews all the new tenants who wish to apply for admission into the building. This screening process is a key element in keeping people who are very likely to be troublemakers from even entering the building. A manager has to make subjective decisions in many instances, but what is at stake is the vitality of a whole neighborhood. A manager collects the rents, makes repairs, pays the taxes and makes sure all the utility bills are paid and the individual units are working. Management also complies with city laws with respect to trash collection and general building and grounds upkeep of the property. Security, a major consideration in urban areas, is maintained by management, and all improvements, repairs and clean-ups, especially after tenants vacate, are the responsibility of management. When tenants are late or refuse to pay rent, management's job is to assess late fees and take tenants to court, if necessary, for payment and/or vacating of the premises. An apartment building is a business and, as such, it is to generate a profit.

Like all businesses, its profit return will be closely tied to how well it is managed. Building owners seldom live in their buildings and often do not even live in the city or state where the property is located. They depend on managers to take care of all their property's concerns, pay the bills and send them their profits. In return for performng their duties, managers get themselves a monthly fee, which is a percentage of the rent collected. They get their fee, in fact, *before* the owner gets his profits. The biggest concern of managers is the hassling with tenants who are now often organized in groups which threaten rent strikes in situations of disagreement. Although apartment managers clearly work for often wealthy White owners, they obviously cannot help anyone if they displease the tenants. In that regard, building managers basically look after virtually everyone's interests. It must also be made clear that there are differences very often between a building manager and a building superintendent. A building "super" often lives in one of the apartments in the building and is the actual handyman that personally does all the repairs and collections. A "super" may work directly for the building owner. Sometimes, however, a "super" works for a management company that manages many buildings for many owners.

Black people will virtually always stand to gain when we own as much as our living space as is possible. But, short of that ideal situation, we stand to gain when we at least manage the space we live in so that it reflects our needs.

Minimum Requirements: Most states require building managers to have real estate licenses but this is not necessary for building superintendents in most cases. After obtaining the license, an individual must take special courses in management, and then market their services to property owners after getting the required experience. Many real estate companies have separate management companies in-house, but one also finds separate companies outside of real estate offices who simply specialize in management. Not only are apartment buildings managed but office buildings, shopping malls, medical buildings, etc. Many White owners view the Black tenant, the Black shopper (shoplifter) as the potential problem; therefore, a professional Black manager would appear to be potentially the type of person who could defuse rather than inflame bad situations. Unfortunately, because of Black folks' historical difficulty in accepting the concept of "Black Authority," Black managers could, in fact, cause more problems than Whites if their professionalism wavers in any way.

Financial Investment Necessary: Most people begin their career by handling the rentals of apartments in a real estate office. This cost is virtually nil because the real estate broker carries all of the overhead. Later, however, if one decides to open one's own apartment or property management company, the usual expenses, rentals and leases associated with opening a professional office would apply. After substantial contracts were acquired, one would need to pay a full-time secretary and assistant managers at the fifteen to twenty-thousand dollar per year salary range.

Financial Possibilities: The fees that building managers charge for managing a building are very varied and depend on a number of factors. I have heard figures of five percent of gross rents for so-called easy jobs and figures as high as twenty percent for problem properties. Naturally, competition and the total array of responsibilities affect the profit percentages. If a single building has 30 apartments renting for $300 per month each, the monthly total would be $9,000. If on average your fee is ten percent, that would make for a monthly income of $900. If you have twenty to thirty buildings of similar size, your monthly gross income would be between $18,000 and $27,000 per month. If your net was say 15% profit and you paid yourself a salary of $30,000 per year, your total yearly compensation would be from $62,000 to $78,000 per year.

A great advantage to people that are involved in this business is that they are very often among the first to know when a building is being sold. Because they are the managers of these properties, they are in a position to buy the properties from the owner themselves and usually on very good financing terms. Who can the owner better trust for steady payments than the person who has been paying him or her all the time?

If the manager does not wish to buy the property but still has a real estate license, they are in a position to list and sell the property and make a very good one-time commission. When the new owner takes over, they are again in the best position to maintain their management contract and continue their monthly income.

For Further Information: Most of the popular real estate books have a section on management. The best single book is probably Dr. Albert Lowery's, *How To Manage Real Estate Successfully In Your Spare Time.*

A lot of insight can be gained by talking to your local brokers and the state real estate commissions and boards usually based in your state capital.

#3.   Home Cleaning Services

The mothers of the readers of this book are perhaps the last generation of Black women who voluntarily filed into White folks homes to do their scrubbing, washing and baby-sitting. As thankful as we are that they subjected themselves to such a role in order to support us and pay for our education, today's Black women have no intention of continuing in that stereotype. Therein lies both the opportunity and the problem of the highly growing field of maid service.

Opportunity lies in the fact that today's liberated woman, single parent households, career and professional women and female property owners have little time and inclination towards traditional housecleaning. The Yuppies, Buppies and their aspirants, while not obsessed with cleanliness as their foreparents were, nevertheless still enjoy the pleasure of an occasionally clean home. The trouble is that their time is at a premium and it is simply not worth their time to do the dusting and scrubbing that is necessary.

They will gladly budget for such services if they can be assured of speed, thoroughness and security. Thus, housecleaning has become an exploding industry and a profitable one for those who are systematic and business-oriented. The problem lies in the fact that good help is still very hard to find. The various forms of unemployment programs, "paid under the table" jobs and the underground economy in general make it difficult for maid service business owners to maintain a stable group of workers. In this sense, their problem and their challenge is much like the owners of fast food restaurants in the ghetto who pay but minimum wages to their constant turnover of employees.

The reasons that this may be a very good business for Blacks are as follows. First, there are a large number of Black families who would pay for the services of regular housecleaners. The neighborhoods where these services are currently concentrated are not the Black neighborhoods, and only sporatically in integrated ones. Therefore, there is a vacuum waiting to be filled by some enterprising Black entrepreneur. Secondly, this business is a rather easy one for Blacks to penetrate the White market. Whereas many Whites may not respect our expertise in computers, law, medicine or engineering, they are very used to seeing us as house servants and cleaners. For a Black person to sell a White on the efficiency of his/her cleaning company is not an impossible sale. A third reason that this is a good business opportunity is because within house cleaning are specializations that one can develop and make even more income. Window washing, rug shampooing, upholstery cleaning and chimney sweeping are all significant sidelines that can generate substantial profits. Light janitorial services and office cleaning are other related enterprises that can lead to commercial contracts.

The secret to today's success in this business is speed and numbers. Rather than one person taking on an entire house, a team of two to four people take on up to ten houses in a day. With tight scheduling, a multiseat van and modern equipment, this is quite feasible. As one's client list grows, expenses can be cut by volume-buying of cleaners and supplies. Although it is never a good idea to minimize the role of business promotion and advertising, maid service is one great business for word of mouth credibility and referrals.

It is important that the maid service owner understand the degree of professionalism, administrative skills, public relations, etc., that are called for in this job is every bit as demanding as other labor-intensive (temporary secretaries, fast-food operations, etc.) enterprises. If your ego won't get in the way, a small fortune could be waiting for you.

Minimum Requirements: It appears that the biggest share of one's money is that which one needs to pay one's personal bills until the cash flow from the business enables one to be self-supporting. The equipment needed for house cleaning is minimal and certainly does not have to be brand new. Many have begun with as little as a hundred dollars.

Financial Opportunities: The money to be made in maid service is dependent not only on the number of regular clients but the quality of clients as well. The wealthier can afford higher rates than urban apartment dwellers. Profit margins of 25 to 30 percent are known to be possible because the overhead is minimal compared to other businesses. There is no need, for example, for clients to come to your office in the normal course of events. Industry figures show that thirty thousand dollars profit on top of a normal manager's salary are common for moderately successful operations.

For Further Information: Several companies offer franchises which cost up to twenty thousand dollars or more. These companies run ads in the back of *Entreprenuer* Magazine, *Venture* and *Inc.* magazine and *Money* magazine. It may be worth your while to write or call them to obtain all their information. After analyzing all the procedures and requirements, one can make up one's mind if it would be in their best interest to join the franchise or use the information to construct one's own operation.

#4. Burglary (and Fire) Alarm Systems

Times have really changed and whether it has been for the better or worse is debatable. Many of us have grandmothers and grandfathers who tell us about days in the south when they could leave home and go to church and leave the front door to the house open, the windows open, with no thought whatsoever to the possibility of being robbed or burglarized. Was it because people were more honest, more religious and more friendly that they didn't steal, or was it because nobody had much in the way of valuables worth stealing? Certainly, television did not program people to want and expect the luxury items that they do today, and it didn't hurt that rural areas made for considerable distances between houses.

In any event, this is a new day and there is a robbery committed about every ten seconds of every hour, every day. Where is the greatest concentration of these robberies? You guessed it—the Black community. Black on Black crime is a great factor in the mutual distrust in our community. Drug use has an incredible effect on the rise of all types of robberies and burglaries. Young people under twenty-five, looking for a quick way to obtain the video set, the stereo system, the computer and jewelry that is constantly paraded before them, are the major culprits in these activities. What is coming out of this has strong social and political consequences, because Blacks with money more than ever are seeking to separate themselves from poorer Blacks. In the past, this phenomenon may have been done for prestige reasons; today, it seems to be motivated strictly as a means of survival.

In this madness, there is a business opportunity. Unfortunately not nearly enough Blacks are being paid to protect us from each other. As the response rates of urban policemen and firemen continue to decline and an attitude of tolerance for crime and arson continue to seep into the mind-set of a community, it will be more and more important for individuals to protect their belongings themselves. As more women leave the home for work, leaving the home empty, daylight burglaries will increase also.

The security field is a strong area of business in that events which bring anger and frustration to the common group actually favor the people in this field and make them richer. As stated earlier, problems are a source of money.

The security field has several parts and there is nothing that says an enterprising person cannot get involved in all of them. The home alarm system market is a tremendously growing field and one where people are prepared to spend a substantial amount of money. Car alarm systems are another huge market, and once you have gained a satisfied client, who is to say you won't help protect every car in the family. The next alarm market consists of business alarms which are tied in to police departments. A higher level of competence is required to handle the commercial alarm market. Fire alarm systems are often tied in to security systems and this is another avenue for profits.

Minimum Requirements: Most certainly there are a series of training programs which aspiring businesspersons must take in order to develop competence in the field. These programs are most often offered by the companies which manufacture or wholesale the various alarms. These companies advertise in the same business opportunity magazines already mentioned or they are listed in the trade journals of the security business which might be found in a business library. Just open the yellow pages under alarms and introduce yourself to the owners of the companies listed. They could very well be the ones that point you in the right direction.

Financial Investment: In the beginning it would seem wise to start the alarm business on a part-time basis. Evenings and week-ends can be used for training, sales and installations. At this rate, inventory needs would be low and a person could easily operate out of their home. When the stage is reached where one is ready to go full time, full office facilities will be needed. A couple thousand dollars ought to be enough for the beginner, but office expenses will vary depending on circumstances. This particular business lends itself to a partnership arrangement rather easily. A mechanically-minded person could do or direct all the installations, while an administrative personality would take care of the purchasing, financing, sales and planning.

Financial Opportunities: In the alarm business, one is making money from both products and services. The alarms generate a profit, the installation cost is padded to cover significant overhead. Car systems cost at least a couple of hundred dollars and sophisticated electronic home systems cost into the thousands. By merely doing two houses and two cars a week, a small operation can gross nearly five thousand dollars, and that is with no commercial work. Normal business profits of 15% above salary could easily net an owner better than fifty thousand dollars per year. Of course, people avoid investing their money for things like alarms unless they are hit with a major tragedy and then they respond after the fact. That is why a sales force is so important. They need to get into the actual homes, give demonstrations, statistics and lean on everyone's desire for security. Of course, good salespeople do not come cheap, and the percentages they require eat heavily into the profits to be made from the alarms. But, like any other business, you make it up on volume.

For Further Information: The telephone book's yellow pages offer the easiest, closest and most immediate sources of reference.

#5. Roller Skating Rink

Virtually every inner city area in the United States has an absence of substantial supermarkets. Many former markets are now boarded up structures and stand abandoned. In these same communities, there is also a great number of youngsters crowded into a relatively small area with inadequate recreational facilities and a minimum of after-school programs. These two factors can be a business bonanza for an enterprising business person with substantial financial backing.

Roller skating is a business that appears to answer a number of problems for the Black community. In the first place, a roller rink has the size to accommodate a large number of kids that often do not have access to facilities for indoor activity. As recreation departments and school budgets are pared down, young people are at a loss to find things to do with their energy. Roller skating is a low-cost form of entertainment and thus is affordable to most people in the community. But on closer inspection, a roller rink is a large clear span building and, as such, it can be made to serve a variety of functions. On any given night, a rink can be a disco, a Karate tourney site, a boxing facility, a theatre for plays, or the site of a gospel concert. In effect, a roller rink can be a full-entertainment center for the entire community, given an innovative program director. A rink can offer exercise programs for the elderly in the day time and serve a tumbling team in the afternoon and return to its rink function by the evening.

The size of the rink can also make it useful to handle very large receptions or even political meetings, if desired.

Minimum Requirements: Developing an attractive rink facility
is a major effort and requires a substantial amount of capital. First, a feasible building needs to be identified. The building needs to have at least ten thousand square feet of floor space free of supporting beams. There needs to be adequate parking space and access to public transportation lines. Both city zoning boards and community groups have to support the idea of a rink in their midst or they can kill the idea quickly. There is no school for one to attend to learn how to run a roller rink, but there are a few persons across the nation who have acted as consultants on the development of new rinks. It is assumed that one would have visited several or more rinks and done a bit of their own research on the topic. One would need not only the normal professionals in pulling of a rink conversion (lawyer, accountant, insurance person, banker) but additional services might be needed from an architect, a sound and light engineer, a designer, etc.

Financial Investment: Opening even a moderate sized roller rink
is a major financial undertaking. A facility needs hundreds of skates,

a giant, level, firm, smooth floor, lockers, a concession area and a highly sophisticated light and sound system. The security and operation of such a building requires a full staff and backups. It would be difficult for such an enterprise to come together, even using a converted building on a lease basis, for less than two hundred thousand dollars. It is highly unlikely that a regular bank would lend this amount of money for something like a roller rink. Why? Because if worse came to worse, the value of the rink could not be obtained by selling off the assets. How fast could one sell three hundred pairs of used roller skates and how much below their original cost would you eventually collect? What do you do with a fifty thousand dollar floor that sits in a building that was boarded up before you opened it and seems destined to be boarded up again? No, banks are not likely to furnish the capital for such an enterprise. This doesn't mean that you shouldn't try. But plan on putting a lot of your own or somebody else's money into this one if you decide to try to pull it off.

Financial Opportunity: The money to be made in a successful roller rink is probably greater than most things that you can name in the Black community. This would be particularly so if you adopted the entertainment center approach rather than concentrated solely on the rink function. Let's understand why there would be so much money. First of all, it is one of the lowest cost entertainment places in the city. The admission fee is less than movies, concerts, amusement parks, nightclubs and dances; therefore, it has broad mass appeal. Secondly, it is a repeat or habit-forming activity. People who skate do so two or more times per week. Thirdly, whereas a movie invites you to eat, one need not do so because you are only going to be sitting down for two hours. In a roller rink, you virtually must eat because the activity builds up hunger. Next is the reality that a rink can have some very long hours, from early a.m. to very late p.m., and it is generating money all of that time. Fifthly, most rinks sell products at retail from a store (a "pro" shop) inside. Profits are not only made from the pro shop but the concession areas, candy machines, video machines, lockers and skate rentals all add to the total haul. If one diversifies the rink and rents it out to others during slow periods, or stages special events, like plays, concerts, etc., the total income just keeps climbing.

The beautiful thing about a rink is that once one gets the up-front costs paid for, the expenses don't increase. You are paid to play music and people can skate without any help from you. Replacing skates here and there, reordering supplies and food are not major financial outlays. A rink is the perfect place to stock the latest inexpensive foods, T-shirts and other items that young people are constantly craving. Because of the low expenses of operating rinks, profit margins have been known to be as high as thirty-five percent. Successful businesses (which concentrated on the rink functions only) have been known to gross from three hundred thousand to a million a year. One hundred thousand dollar profits are quite possible, over and above a salary.

For Further Information: There are about three thousand, five hundred roller rinks in the nation. The best means for getting information is to visit with some rink owners and ask to examine any industry materials that they might have.

#6. Independent School

In the mid-1960's, when the federal government made it clear that they were going to enforce a policy of integrated public schools in the South, many White Southerners banded together to open private schools. In looking at that development twenty years later the interesting thing is not so much their decision to form their own schools so much as their ability to develop so many schools so quickly.

For the last fifteen years at least, there has been a constant chronicling of the horrors and inadequacies of the public school system and of inner city public schools, particularly. But in that period of time, the attempts by the Black community and by Black businesspeople to actually develop and nurture their own private institutions has been rather feeble. When institutions are developed, they serve basically the primary grades, so that when the junior high and high school years arrive, the youngsters have to go back to the negative conditions of public schools anyway.

Black people have a tremendous supply of people trained as educators, administrators, trainers and the like. There appears to be no reason why every major metropolitan area of about two hundred thousand Black folks cannot support at least one substantial private school. The battle to improve or save public education must go on and will go on. But a self-determined people who do not have to face the responsibility of launching space satellites or curing cancer or cleaning up pollution ought to at least be able to provide one decent school for their young.

These schools would probably cater to the middle class, not because of class snobbery but out of economic necessity. Education is expensive.

In order to justify the expense, private schools need to offer the kind of useful information that is not covered or is covered inadequately in most public schools. Young people can be taught early the importance of money management and credit. They can cover computer skills and practice research skills, because as adults they are not necessarily challenged on how much information they have stored up in their head but are challenged on how to find the answers, information, people, organizations, agencies and institutions they need. Students ought to learn about sales and its importance as the central aspect of virtually any enterprise. Furthermore, students need to be brought before video cameras and taught how to present themselves to the public.

Such schools need not concentrate solely on college preparation, but could just as easily concentrate their efforts on developing independent and motivated individuals who would like to pursue important and lucrative positions in life, not requiring the college degree. It should not automatically mean, however, that that student would be totally unprepared for college should they decide to attend.

Finally, we need a place where people can be drilled on the skills and preparation of test-taking. Since standard tests are such a part of the process of being measured against the norm, we should study the things which have proven to improve test scores. Clearly, it has been proven that it is not merely the memorization of additional information.

Minimum Requirements: Every state has a department of education which lists the criteria an institution must meet to be declared a certified school. These requirements must be met in order to assure parents that your enterprise is legitimate and accredited. Meeting these minimum standards will be no simple task.

Financial Investment: The investment necessary to even start a small model school will be substantial and will require very extensive planning. In addition to finding a suitable building and bringing it up to standards, the school must be furnished and staffed. Usually this is done by a large fund-raising effort which includes the submission of proposals to foundations and special grant agencies. A viable school must certainly be designed to take advantage of both nonprofit and profit-making opportunities. I have seen instances where aspects of an institution are charted as nonprofit enterprises and are allowed to pursue regular fund-raising efforts. These same institutions, however, have a profit aspect which allows them to sell, promote and organize profitable ventures to support activities which complement the nonprofit aspects of the institution. Obviously, a strong legal mind is necessary to structure an entity so that all potential bases can be tapped.

Tuition fees are obviously a part of the working budget of any school, but good schools are in a position to offer many services to the community. Why couldn't a school, its students and employees offer the following services to the community and the private business sector:

1. *Bookstore*: sell all items normally found in commercial bookstores.
2. *Printing*: serve personal and business needs.
3. *Restaurant*: offer morning and lunch meals.
4. *Computer Services*: serve small businesses.
5. *Typing Services*: serve individuals and small businesses.
6. *Concert & Guest Lecture Promotion*: open to the public at normal retail prices.
7. *Recreational Services*: Public use for a normal price during those hours when not used by students (tennis, swimming, racketball, etc.).
8. *Flea Market Facility*: rental profits for weekend use.
9. *Automotive Repair*: this is a common trade school service.
10. *Arts & Crafts Show*: encourage student artists to market their creations to serve the school's needs and their own.
11. *Local Newspaper*: school newspapers can be expanded to take in local ads and news.

If you study this list you will note that many colleges and community colleges are already marketing these services to the general public. What I am proposing then is that a private high school can and should operate more along a college mold. This will not only help the institution economically, but would add greatly to the maturity of the students and allow them to have a much earlier exposure to the real world.

Financial Possibilities: It would most certainly take a great deal of time for most people to adjust to the idea of a privately-owned school. Private school has never meant individual ownership or school for the purpose of wealth accumulation for a single individual. Thus, the structure of the type of school suggested here would probably be a corporation with investors and a board of directors. After the institution is on sound financial footing, the major stock holder-president is entitled not only to a salary better than poorly paid public school personnel (principals average about thirty to thirty-five thousand a year for nine months work) but other perks that come with corporation compensation. I would imagine that a total salary package of around fifty to sixty thousand dollars a year and the freedom and joy to implement sound educational practices would constitute business success. Would you?

For Further Information: Few books discuss the idea of a privately-owned high school. Such an idea would almost certainly have to be individually handcrafted and designed to meet the educational standards, regulations, politics and public opinion of the area. Thus, personal research, especially of the privately-owned trade schools in the area, is a key aspect of this research. The yellow pages are the key to finding local trade schools.

#7. Financial Broker

By far, the most common question and concern that I encounter among Black people seeking to go into business is the issue of up-front or expansion financing. Black folk seem to be saying, "Hell, we know we can be successful in our business; we just want to know where we can get the money." As this book has tried to point out, many times people think they are ready to take on the business world when maybe they aren't. But, without question, the problem of Blacks getting money for their business is a very real one.

If, as I have strongly stated, we as people do not get proper exposure to the money and business world, it should not be surprising that we have a limited perspective as to sources for business financing. But even beyond that, there is a serious question of whether we do the right thing when *we have located the right funding*. Let me explain.

When Black people are denied a request or privilege, we almost automatically assume that it was due to racism. Certainly, this has been an accurate assumption more times than not in our history here in America and certainly it appears that way many times today. But, in many instances, we are denied requests simply because we do not do the right thing. Sometimes, we have the wrong information to begin with, we ask the wrong person, we ask at the wrong time, we don't complete the paperwork, we do the paperwork incorrectly, or we commit a host of other errors. With regard to being denied a loan, let's look at what could go wrong in the negotiations, which you may not ever learn because they may not tell you.

1. The amount of money asked for is too small for it to be considered a business loan.
2. The loan is for too long a period of time.
3. The loan is for an enterprise that lenders have found to be unprofitable (they've lost money on that kind of loan already).
4. The paper work is incorrect.
   a. You have unrealistic sales projections.
   b. You have unrealistic business expenses.
   c. You have unrealistic profit margins, etc.
5. The business you are interested in (or the location where you seek to operate) is already over-saturated with that kind of business.

The number of ways a bank or lender can say no is beyond imagination, but it still ends in a no. Black people's weakest bargaining position is not only insufficient collateral to back a loan, but the fact that they cannot claim to have large amounts of money in virtually any bank. A bank can only lend if it has money and it can only have money if people make deposits. Even though Blacks have billions of dollars passing through their hands every month, they do not save much of this money. Thus, many Blacks often cannot prove to a bank that they are "owed" a better than even break because their holdings in that bank are less than substantial. This, of course, doesn't mean that banks therefore have a license to discriminate against Blacks. It does mean, however, that Blacks cannot negotiate from a position of strength on questionable deals. A money broker, then, is a very much needed professional in our community.

A money broker gets paid to do all the things right that an individual may do wrong. A money broker not only contacts the right institution and the right person, but he or she may know that person personally and have that person's respect. If a contact cannot help, they may suggest someone who will. Paperwork, projections, market studies, etc., are the things that brokers go over, because *their* name is being associated with the loan and they cannot make a living and gain respect if they come in looking dumb. For every approved loan, a broker gets automatic profit in the pocket.

A money broker follows banking and lending trends the way fans follow their favorite sports teams. Additionally, a money broker has a network of lenders who finance businesses that regular banks would not touch. These lenders may ask for more security and higher interest rates, but their risk may very well justify what they are asking. A money broker, then, is a hired consultant who assists people with the potential to obtain funds to *actually* obtain them. They cannot, in most instances, get money for someone who does not have something to lose or give up.

If we can develop a national resource group of money brokers in the Black community, may possibilities would seem to exist. More businesses, employment, housing and products would be available in our community. But not only that, with more common knowledge of what lenders look for, we would have a lot more people "positioning" themselves for loans. More people would arrange their affairs so as to qualify for a loan prior to the time the money was actually needed.

Black money brokers could also be of great assistance in helping Black investment groups invest in Black businesses. In other words, money brokers could start us and help us in lending money to each other. Unless Black folk feel comfortable with the idea of lending money to each other, can we really complain about what others are not doing for us?

Minimum Requirements: There are several companies (listed in the back of some of the magazines mentioned before) which offer the general public the opportunity to get involved in the business of money brokering. Companies in this business often advertise in the business opportunity section of Sunday newspapers.

On paper, there doesn't appear to be much in the way of professional requirements. However, because of the extreme doubts held for Blacks about business and finance, I suggest that the aspiring money broker learn the fundamentals not only about business but also about finance and banking. One can simply go into a college bookstore and purchase the textbooks used in the college courses dealing with these topics; no enrollment or tuition payment is necessary. Like most situations, working under an expert for as long as you need to seems the surest way to learn the field.

Financial Investment: This field is an easy one to start on a part-time basis. Perhaps here Black corporate employees can use their accounting, management, marketing and M.B.A. training to start something on their own while still enjoying corporate benefits.

Operating out of a small home office with an answering service, one can meet clients and lenders at their place of business or in restaurants. If you decide to go full-time, a small professonal office will probably be all you need. Because a squeaky-clean image and professionalism will be important, quality is important and must be reflected in anything you do.

Financial Possibilities: There are two ways of getting paid in this business. The first way is to charge an hourly rate (from $50 to $150 per hour) for your professional services. In this capacity you assist your client in preparing their business plan, making recommendations on the best means of presenting themselves, their business, their needs and their total business offer. When the consulting is done and you get paid, the client will present the loan package to his or her own lending contacts, family members or use their attorney's contacts. You will have been paid in this instance for your time, not for results.

The second way to get paid is to take the client completely through the preparation stage through to actually receiving the loan. At that point, you get paid whatever you were successful in negotiating. Loan fees are counted in "points," with each point equalling a percentage point of the loan. Small loans usually merit large percentages of up to ten percent. Very large loans can be as small as a half point. For example, if I charge ten points on a twenty thousand dollar loan, I stand to make two thousand dollars for my efforts (the client will get eighteen thousand dollars but will repay twenty thousand to the lender, plus interest). If I help someone obtain a two million dollar loan and I've charged two points, I stand to get forty thousand dollars for that one loan transaction.

The chances are very likely that once you get into this business, you are going to open doors to whomever wishes to enter and pay for your services. At that point, there is the danger to the Black community of losing a good person again. Why? Because Blacks seldom come through the door asking to borrow a million or more dollars. They do not have that much equity to borrow against. However, Whites borrow millions of dollars every day. If you as a businessperson have a limited amount of time and resources (we all do) and you have Whites whose average request is for seven hundred thousand, who is going to get most of your attention? How much more profit will you get by riding herd on the White applications than you will by keeping track of the Blacks? Although this seems at first like a Black and White issue, it is not. For the same amount of paperwork, phone calls, personal contacts, etc., you get vastly different sums of money out the other side. If you can see this clearly, then you can also see the bank's position when they turn us down.

Black people must change the scale of their thinking if they are to grab the attention of the people they need. As sad as it might seem, in business "small" often means failure. And whereas all businesses start out as small businesses, we set our sights so low that ours could be called super-small businesses. Most lenders have doubts about a super-small business. They don't believe it will impress customers (the market), so they automatically will not back it. Black people have to plan businesses that will be big enough to satisfy everybody involved: lenders, brokers, customers, news media, suppliers, employees and themselves.

For Further Information: See minimum requirements.

#8. Travel Agency

The number one complaint that Black people have against Black businesses is that their prices are always higher than their White counterparts. In spite of the extensive explanations for why such price differences exist, the bottom line is that the poorest sector of America is expected to pay their own businesspersons more money for products that they can buy cheaper elsewhere. This problem will continue to plague many Black businesses for some time. Fortunately, there are some businesses where everybody's price is the same. The travel agency business is one such business. This means that Black agents (as in real estate) stand on equal footing with Whites in terms of selling the services one uses in traveling.

Statistics indicate that Black Americans spend billions of dollars a year in the travel industry. A large part of this amount, about two and half billion, is spent by the thousands of our people in business and the professions who attend the more than one hundred and fifty conferences given each year by the various Black professional organizations. Currently, there are relatively few Blacks in the travel agency business, and if we are to gain our share of profits from this business, we must take advantage of the opportunities. There are several reasons why this business is recommended, in addition to the equal price policy already mentioned.

First, it requires a small amount of training to get started and only a modest amount of capital to open your own operation after you get started. Secondly, the scope of the business is more than simply booking airplane or train tickets but includes cruises, bus trips and tours, hotel rooms and car rentals. An owner would be interested in gaining the business of already active travelers and also "selling" those who do not travel on the idea of travel. One also wants to plan their clients' business trips as well as their family vacations. This brings us to the third reason this business merits strong consideration, the corporate accounts.

As you are aware, the nation's businesses are occasionally under pressure to utilize and patronize Black and minority businesses. Our problems have been that we often could not provide an essential service that they use or we could not provide that product or service at a competitive price. A travel service agency cures both problems, so that it would be an excellent business for that businessperson who would rather deal with corporations than individual clients. Fortunately, in this business you do not have to choose; one can serve both. Another major reason to look into this business is because of its fantastic growth. Travel, vacations and tourism is one of the top five industries in the nation. Everyone within reason cuts loose and splurges on a get-away at some time of the year. As air fares come down, more people are leaving the car at home, flying and renting a new car when they get to their destination. An agent stands to make money on both counts. Agents get paid in travel as well as money in this business. Therefore, whereas an ordinary person pays off their credit cards for eight months for the one splurge they took in the summer, agents often take Spring, Summer, Fall and Winter vacations and have very few bills, because so much of the vacations are provided virtually free.

Minimum Requirements: Travel agents are much like real estate agents in that they take a short course and pass a qualifying exam in order to work for an agency owner. After they have demonstrated the organizing skills to develop a trip package and the public relations and sales ability to get new customers, only money and basic professional and state requirements stand between them and the opening of their own agency.

Financial Investment: After taking the required training, an agent merely has to report to work and find a desk under an agency owner.

When the time to open one's own agency arrives, the twenty thousand or so dollars that it costs to open virtually any professional office will be required. An extensive computer and telephone line hook-up is essential.

Financial Possibilities: Travel agents receive between five and fifteen percent of the total sum spent by their clients on travel, hotel and car rentals. Agency owners receive half of the fees of all the agents they have working under them. Thus, the newcomer receives about eight percent of total sales made. This can amount to as much as thirty thousand or more dollars a year, but not without significant business or group clients. Agency owners naturally make more, not only because they have their old line of customers and constant referrals, but because they keep half the fees of the agents working in their offices. Their many free pleasure trips are gravy.

Black agency owners will find several problems. One, their individual clients will spend virtually all of their travel money from June through August. Few Blacks take real vacations in the winter or spring; thus, a cash flow problem is a real possibility. Secondly, most Black business and convention travel is also concentrated during that same time period, the Summer. Thirdly, corporations have been travelling for decades so it will not be easy to break the hold of long-term relationships, especially if you are just learning about the business *and* the clients. But the challenge awaits us. In the White agency world, successful but rather small agent owners have been known to make over a hundred thousand per year.

For Further Information: Visit agencies in your area and pick up brochures supplied by the many vocational and private schools teaching a travel agent course.

Summary

The suggested businesses contained here share several things in common which I think should be noted. First, most of them concern themselves with the utilization of resources or interests that are already ours. Black people already travel, we already live in apartments, we already have large abandoned buildings available to us and we already buy alarm systems to protect our personal and real property. The issue is whether we as Black people are profiting by the things that we already buy, have or do. Secondly, virtually all of the businesses suggested allow us to capture some of the majority market dollar. Black people will not have more money as a group if we just shuffle the 7.6 percent of the nation's economy back and forth to each other. In order for twelve percent of the population to get twelve percent of the national income, more money must be obtained from outside our community. Thirdly, most of the businesses suggested here require rather small amounts of investment dollars (except a couple) and/or can be started on a part-time basis. This is important for people who are looking to make a smooth transition from the 9 to 5 job to full business ownership. Another characteristic you will note here is the minimum formal education needed to engage in these businesses (excepting private school).

The final thing that these business suggestions have in common is the promise of future growth. There is nothing here that will not grow in the future, especially if a competent Black person runs them professionally. Do you realize how few property managers, travel agents, financial brokers, alarm system specialists or roller rink owners are Black? These fields are not only wide open, but businesses which utilize similar resources are likewise open.

GENERAL SUGGESTIONS FOR BLACK BUSINESS

If you feel slightly confused with understanding the absolute philosophy of this presentation, it is somewhat understandable. On one hand I am saying serve Black people, and on the other I'm saying reach out to White customers. On one hand I clearly understand Black people's habits, values, expectations and interpretations, but on the other I recommend doing things the way "White Folks" do them. On one hand I chastise Blacks for being so involved with multi-national corporations, and then on the other I turn around and recommend Black business do "bidness" with these same corporations whenever possible (obviously the more Black corporate executives we have in these corporations, the better, supposedly, are our chances of doing business with these giants).

If you are wondering "where I'm coming from," the truth is I'm coming from everywhere. You see, people who are big in their thinking and who have traveled and studied different people and cultures have all concluded exactly the same thing, that there are lessons and skills to be learned everywhere. As the world shrinks thanks to satellite communications and jumbo jets, the entire world, not just America, has become a melting pot. No people in the "modern" world can safely feel comfortable being totally immersed in and guided by their own cultural traits. If someone comes up with what has proven to be better, you might profit by checking it out. Organ transplants are intercultural and interracial. Everybody would prefer to have a heart, kidney, liver and blood—even if it came from somewhere else. I am for the service of Black people but I am not one to say (as I've heard so many times) *all* the answers are within *us*. All the answers are distributed among the world's people and I, for one, don't mind borrowing what I need to get where I want to go. Japan, perhaps, is the model in this regard. They were able to recover from two atomic bombs and all the devastation of the Second World War because they decided they were going to study everybody's techniques and integrate them into Japanese culture whenever appropriate. And if Japanese culture was to drastically change from what it had been, so be it; they would emerge stronger, richer and more confident. I think there is a lesson here for all of us.

This chapter has as its purpose the presentation of general ideas that do not fit neatly into the previous chapters but which, on the whole, have merit. There might possibly be some small repetition here with previously expressed ideas, and I hope that will be tolerated. I have found that repetition is a key to learning and hopefully you will too.

Shopping as a Total Experience

For the owner of a retail operation, the desire is to see customers pouring in constantly and the cash register steadily filling up. And as much as all of us owners want to see that, we best make it our business to constantly try to see things from the *customer's point of view*. From the customer's point of view, there is "convenience" shopping and "experience" shopping. Convenience shopping is usually limited to very basic food, hardware, household or automobile items, where you run in and out with the items as fast as possible. The competition in this field is tremendous precisely because the items are so basic. Many Black folk, however, are doing well in food, auto supply and general purpose stores. Many of us, on the other hand, market items which we think are rather special or unique. Many of these retailers are at a loss to understand why our inventories are not moving. My hunch is that you may be trying to sell an "experience" purchase item from a "convenience" location. What do I mean? I mean that today, perhaps more than ever, people (and probably more women and children than men) go shopping not just to buy a particular item but to experience a total sense of entertainment. Shopping malls function not only for the purpose of concentrating a variety of retail operations (from shoes to paint to computers), but to actually set up a total environment where customers can browse and become totally educated as to what's out on the market. Consumers *learn what to want* and plan the next buying spree as a direct result of today's browsing. Mall operators are very skillful in offering something for everybody. At any given time among the waterfalls, reflecting pools and gliding escalators, they present amusement rides, clowns, Santa Claus, Mimes, artists of all kinds or special collectibles. By drawing thousands of people to a location, providing a dozen or more low cost restaurants, movies, etc., a distinct social atmosphere is developed where boy can meet girl. Whether malls offer fashion shows or not, the clientele of certain expensive malls become a live fashion experience. For Black people who do not like where they live or how they live, and who tire of television, the mall is the place to see how the other America lives in a very real way. Their willingness to pay more for an item in the mall than in your corner dress shop is their way of saying, "I'm not just a ghetto child; I belong (or will belong) to this world as well. I deserve what is here and I will pay the price to prove that I deserve what is here." Shopping—probably among all people but probably particularly among Blacks—is a psychological game where money is used to try to soothe an unsatisfied spirit. When people are bored, they go to the mall. When they are depressed, they go to the mall. When they are lonely or even happy, they go to the mall. The ramifications of this reality for Black business is significant. You must not only be more than just Black to attract your target clientele, but apparently having a convenient location, good prices and service may not be enough either. If your business operation is not located in the environment that they seek when it is time to shop, you may just have to write off a portion of your target population. Ideally, you may want to shoot for a place of business in both the community and the mall. Perhaps the day is not too far off when Black bankers, designers, business people and political leaders can get together and develop attractive malls right near where we live.

Advertising and Promotion

The people who make money in business in America are the promoters. The people who can get the attention of the public, charm them with a phrase, a jingle or joke, and then direct them to a particular business establishment. These are the people who are making a killing in the world of business. Promotion, promotion, promotion. Hype, hype, hype. The world of business is run by advertisers and promoters who grab the attention of the public and place in the minds of the public what they want them to believe about a product and the place of business that sells the product. The job of the government is to watch to make sure no particular company goes overboard (false advertising).

How can I be so sure that this is the way it is, you may ask. Well, think about this. Just about everybody has eaten a McDonald's hamburger at some time in their life. And in the same breath, I can say that just about every person that has eaten this hamburger can, with a little effort, make a better hamburger in their own kitchen. The average McDonald's grosses about 1.3 million dollars a year. The average McDonald's in the Black community grosses about 1.7 million dollars in a year. Do you think people buy because it is such a great hamburger? Do you think the people buy because the high school kids there are such great salespeople? Do you think you could collect 1.7 million dollars if you had a hamburger stand at the exact same spot with your better tasting burger? I hope you are honest and answered *no* to all these questions. People buy from McDonald's for many reasons, but not because they have the best burgers in the world. One of the major reasons that people buy from them is because the place is promoted and hyped again, again and again. It's like a disc jockey who plays a record that you don't like, but he plays it so often that you learn to like it; you start to sing it and eventually you may buy it. This, ladies and gentlemen, is called programming.

Programming is the result of advertising and promotion. Over 50,000 million dollars (50 billion) is spent on advertising and promotion each year. This is what helps business succeed.

But, if I were to point out the greatest single drawback of all Black businesses in terms of their failure to get Black customers, I would say it was their dismal, almost invisible presence in the world of advertising and promotion. They are not even in the game.

Let me give you an example. Go to your library or den and pick up six issues of Ebony Magazine, Jet Magazine, Essence Magazine and any other Black magazine that you care to. Open the magazines and count the number of ads in each issue. Then, go back and try to figure out how many of those ads were placed by Black-owned companies. What you will find is that, even though Ebony and Jet are perhaps the most widely distributed and widely read Black magazines in the history of the universe, Black businesses still rarely use them to advertise their products. Now this does not hold true for the beauty and hair care Black business people. They are the exception. They use the medium to get to our people. But that's it. And understand that this is what is happening today, 1985, after thirty-five years of struggle to get these magazines as established as they are. Realistically, without car, liquor and cigarete ads, there would be no Black magazines as we know them in this country today. And for 28 million people, that is sad.

Go to a first class magazine stand or store and look at all the various papers and publications. Notice what a small portion the Black publications take up on the stand. Understand how much advertising is in all the magazines and papers that you see. Try to imagine it. Then look at the three or five Black publications that you see there and understand how extremely few of the 600,000 Black businesses in America are advertising even in those.

That, my friend, should give you some idea of where we are in the advertising game. If you watch television, you know that the Black-owned companies that advertise there are very few. What about billboards on the highway? Surely, Black folk are sophisticated enough to put their business on a wall of wood. Yet, any observer can see that Black-owned companies rarely use these media, and those that do are almost always the hair care companies. The rest of Black American business has a long, long way to go. Many of us have not even made the yellow pages, and that is about the thickest book (with the thinnest pages) in America. Black business people *have* managed to project their images in Black newspapers and on Black radio. But as we enter the end of the 20th century, it is past the time where we need to broaden our message media.

What I'm saying, ladies and gentlemen, is that the secret to business success is to get the people in your store. They are not going to merely come to your store just because it's there.

Obviously, advertising is expensive, and a business must be large or profitable enough to not only advertise but to respond to advertising success. Many small enterprises are not at that level of development yet. The answer for these enterprises may lie in promotion, which is not only cheaper than advertising but is almost always more effective as well. Let's examine promotion.

Most major metropolitan areas have one or two Black T.V. programs and some talk radio shows. If you are knowledgeable about your business, you can apply to be on some of these shows to talk about your area of expertise. Sometimes you approach the subject backwards. For example, let's say you are a carpenter. You go on the radio show talking about home repairs you can do yourself at little or no cost. You ought to be able to do this. Now, you might think, well, if I get people to do all the work themselves, I won't make any money or get any calls. False! You will get plenty of calls. Why? Because people will assume that if you are good enough to get on radio, you must be good. And if you are helping people save money, you must be reasonably priced yourself. And if you come across as a regular guy helping people out and you are on the radio, you must be honest. So even though you are giving free advice on how people can get by without you—the result will be increased credibility and recognition, which means more calls, more business and more money. Your cost is zero. In fact, if enough people call up or write, they will probably rerun the program again.

Many businesses are in a position to do this if they can offer some new insight into their business. You might think, well, I'm not the best in my field. I shouldn't be on the air. It doesn't matter. The best people are too busy to get on the air; they won't ask for the spot. Besides, the radio personality probably won't know who the best is anyway.

The same technique can be used in newspapers, especially Black newspapers. If you write up an advice column or article, and seek no money for it, and it carries some good points, chances are the local Black paper will print it exactly as you wrote it. You can end the article with, "For other free information contact Smith's Carpentry Shop." This allows readers to get back to you directly for advice or business.

Offer to do workshops for Real Estate Seminars or Adult Education classes at the high school. You want people to think of your name when they have a carpentry problem, period! It doesn't matter that they remember it from the radio show, the t.v., the newspaper or a workshop, as long as they call. Right now, what many business people do is merely hand out their cards. Somehow, they expect you to hold on to this card and 300 other ones that you have forever. And if, after 18 months, you use a service very similar to theirs, they will accuse you of not supporting Black business. Do they know that you have been hit with about 7,000 different advertising and promotion messages in that 18 months. You haven't seen their business card in over a year.

The most common excuse I hear from business people about promotion is the lack of time they have for such an effort. Sometimes this is valid but many times it is not. The thing that keeps many Blacks from promotion is their discomfort at drawing attention to themselves. Not only do they dislike drawing attention to themselves, but they often dislike other people who draw attention to themselves. When Muhammad Ali used to brag and boast about his looks and abilities, Black people almost as much as Whites used to want to see the bigmouth get beat. They wanted a quiet humble champ like Floyd Patterson or Joe Louis. But from a business point of view, Ali made more money for himself and other fighters because of his promoting skills. Today, though he is retired, Ali still makes money promoting various products and causes.

The value of advertising and promotion goes beyond planting the *name* of your product or service in the mind of your customer. It also is to promote the *image* you want. When people buy your product or service, they are also buying the image that they associate with the product or service.

Individual business people have problems getting their share of Black customers because of the overall image that Black businesses have in general. Of all the businesses belonging to specific racial groups, none have a worse image than Black business. Therefore, even if Black customers remembered the names and places where Black businesses were located, these same businesses would still have a tremendous need for advertising and promotion in order to change the *image* of those businesses.

Sometimes we also have to face a hard and cold reality. Many Blacks will only support a Black-owned business when that business is good enough for Whites to be interested enough to enter. Blacks have been hit with the idea of Black inferiority so hard that to some a place is not real, is not legitimate, unless it has been approved by the majority population. Their reasoning is, if Whites come here, the place must be clean enough, fair enough, and good enough, otherwise they would not come here. And if it is good enough for them, then it will now be all right for me too. It is not your true role as a businessperson to change social and psychological attitudes; at least, not directly anyway. It may be time for you to get the crossover sales. Crossover in the music industry is when a musical group of one race gets heavy air play and records sales from people of the other race. For instance, Hall and Oates have a very heavy Black following, while Michael Jackson and Donna Summer have strong White supporters. As a businessperson you may want to consider changing your business around to appeal to White clientele, while serving your current Black customers in the same friendly manner. What you might find in getting a few White faces in your establishment each day is that you'll pick up some brand new Black ones as well. This is business.

Changing Parochial Views

One of the common principles that "motivational" books commonly advise is to "think big." My only problem with such advice is that without clear definition, thinking big doesn't mean much to me. What it could mean is to avoid what I label parochial or narrow views in the carrying on of one's business. Have you ever noticed that if a White person and a Black person start up similar businesses in their basements or garages, that one will designate their enterprise as national, American, universal, statewide, etc. The other person, the Black one, will name their business Westside, Southside or Community (as in Community Grocer, Inc.). What this suggests is that even though both persons may be beginning similar kinds of businesses, one person has already decided that their vision includes doing business in the whole nation or at least the state. The other person's vision is limited to serving only the Westside (a region that may be the poorest area in the city).

When a person gears up their whole operation to serve just a part of a town, the "image" of that business is usually more hindered than helped. You are telling lenders and investors in your business that regardless of how good your idea is, you only see yourself operating within the confines of the community that you live in. This is not an incentive for people to lend or invest in that business. Black people need to start thinking how perhaps they can start an idea, test it in a certain market and then seek business opportunities in any market that compares with the successful model. Marketing statistics abound in advertising companies and marketing organizations. The same tools that allow other businesses to penetrate our communities are available for us to penetrate other communities.

If Black businesses are to develop strength, stability and employees, they must seek to serve wherever their service is needed and serve all who are willing and able to pay. The reason that Blacks advertise so little in national publications, Black or otherwise, is because so very few Black enterprises are national. With so few national Black enterprises, it is difficult for us to develop our own "name brands" and develop the image of successful business people. Listed below are some concepts that can help us stretch our idea of who or where our market is.

A. MAIL ORDER SALES

It is quite clear that it is much easier to say "expand beyond your community" than to actually do so. The reason most people think that way is because their concept of expansion usually includes opening a branch store at a new location. Whereas this may be an eventually desirable and affordable thing to do, almost anyone can expand their customer base by using some sort of mail order concept. It is very important that Black business people understand that there are thousands upon thousands of mailing lists that people can rent from mailing list brokers. If you wanted a list of boat owners in Mississippi, or female owners of million dollar businesses in Iowa, or people who read Time magazine in North Dakota, there is a list to rent with specific names. Buying lists is more difficult than renting them. Either way, one can make one's products known to whomever one wishes if one feels that there is interest and a market for the product. Mailing list brokers can discuss your business with you and help you choose the right list of folks.

B. COLORLESS BUSINESSES

There are some types of businesses which are virtually colorless, meaning that it is unimportant what color the owner is and no one stops to wonder. If you are a cigarette smoker, for example, you probably use cigarette machines from time to time. It is very likely that you couldn't care less if the person who eventually collects all those quarters is White, Black, Oriental or Other. All you really care about is if the right pack of cigarettes comes down when you pull the handle. That's all anybody cares about. Black people must get some kind of handle on the colorless businesses that service the entire nation. Vending machines are, of course, a prime example. It is not an easy field to break into and it requires a substantial amount of start-up capital in most circumstances. Out of twenty-eight million people, someone among us should acquire a portion of that market. Mail order companies, mentioned earlier as an aid to market expansion, is also a colorless business. People simply note the brochures, products, prices and send checks or credit card numbers to distant addresses. Who owns the company or where the company is located is not a factor at all in terms of purchases.

Telemarketing is a new business concept that is spreading nationwide. A group of people (or machines) man telephones and call a list of predetermined names. A pleasant pitch is then made for a well-known product and the person on the other end is billed later for their purchase. Like most sales situations, it is a numbers game. A certain percentage of people will buy if the price or the special attraction is appealing. The telephone is a less threatening way for people to communicate, and, here again, there is less concern about the race of the caller, even when they are recognizable. It is definitely a possibility for Black enterprises to penetrate neighborhoods that they cannot get access to physically.

Franchises are, by and large, colorless businesses. When you think of franchises, you think only of the product, not the owner. Regardless of whether it's chicken or carmel chip cookies, the focus is on getting that fine tasting product you had last month in another town, into your mouth today at home. Franchises also cover a great territory outside of fast food. Printing, business consulting and candle shops all have been known to be offered as franchise operations. Chances are, whatever you are interested in, there is a franchise offered, and in most cases they will help you do everything necessary to get started, including help in financing. Blacks will patronize Black franchisors very heavily because it answers all their needs. Under the best conditions, Blacks would like to patronize a business that has a Black owner, a convenient location, basically low prices, well-known national brands and the special sales, contests, giveaways, etc., that they have had pumped at them through television. A Black franchise owner is the perfect answer to these preferred conditions. White consumers will focus on the same basic desires and the race of the owner will hardly be a factor. Product, service and price uniformity are major reasons for this.

Multi-Level Marketing is an excellent colorless business situation that many Blacks are jumping on all over the country. Multi-level marketing is a business situation where you become the direct distributor and salesperson of a product. You make money by selling that product as a representative of a particular company. However, your major purpose is to involve other people in the business through a system of sponsorship. When you build a sales organization, you collect a percentage of the sales of all the people in your sales organization. Now in this situation, Black business people often are not given support by their friends and relatives.

But often the product being sold does not relate to the Black community or it is priced higher than what the Black community feels is justified.

Fortunately for many Blacks, they don't necessarily need a Black clientele. They can share the business opportunity with the kinds of people that the program was designed for in the first place—Middle Class Whites. In this way, some Black business people are earning substantial incomes based on the work, network and sales efforts of people that they might not ever have had occasion to know otherwise.

C. INTERNATIONAL SALES

One of the things that make music and movie superstars what they are is the fact that their products sell all over the world. Fashion designers, writers, artists, etc., are able to strike a nerve not only in their own country but in people worldwide. But one doesn't have to be a superstar to market their products overseas. Thousands of people sell their products every day. Black Americans must identify those nations where their products would appeal to the native population. As wealthy as the United States is, it contains less than twenty percent of the world's wealth. As a people trying to gain a grip on our economic destiny, it would help tremendously if we didn't have to depend strictly on our country's resources. Success in international sales requires a special effort of study and discussions with bankers who handle such matters.

Without question, the Black business community needs to get a new idea of its possibilities. The standard store on the corner is but one way of reaching your customers. There are a number of ways that the modern businessperson can use to penetrate markets that do not lie in close proximity to the actual place of business.

Black Chambers of Commerce

The drive that many individuals have shown to start and develop their business is a prime requirement for business success. However, it becomes very obvious rather soon that working in isolation has its limitations. Individual effort can only get one so far so fast. The White community very long ago responded to this reality by developing a Chamber of Commerce. These business organizations have served business owners and leaders in many capacities. Chamber meetings are a general informational exchange medium where companies find out what each other are doing and planning to do. They also serve as places where the local government explains its agenda to the business community in an effort to get its support. The business community has an opportunity to make critical judgments of governmental plans before the ideas are exposed to the general public. If it is clearly in the business community's interest for a certain law or policy to be put into effect, chambers of commerce can take an offensive posture and advocate what they want. Behind the scenes, chamber members help each other by sharing the kind of inside information on contacts and resources that enables companies to squeeze out that crucial extra five percent profit at the end of the year. The public's awareness of chambers of commerce varies from knowledgeable to total ignorance. The general perception, however, is that business people are shrewd. The public grows to have even more respect for the business community because it is in fact an organized community through these chambers of commerce.

All of this points to why it only makes sense for Black businesses in metropolitan areas to organize themselves into groups similar to chambers of commerce. The Black community needs to have reasons to respect their business owners, and few things will generate this respect more than seeing the business owners organized and helping each other. Collective efforts to get Blacks to support their businesses are probably more likely to succeed than many individual efforts. Certainly, the power of promotion and advertising can be more easily generated from an organized group than from many individual borderline businesses. A Black chamber of commerce need not mean that members will not attend regular chamber meetings. On the contrary, attendance at regular chamber meetings can help Black chamber members form their agenda and strategies for maneuvering in the general business community. An organized business body could also help push borderline businesses to an acceptable standard of operation, and undoubtedly would influence some of the treatment that Black businesses receive in the finance community. Fortunately, Black chambers of commerce are already in existence in a few cities. Hopefully, the growth of these groups will not only continue, but their effectiveness will grow as well.

Reinvesting Profits

Discipline is the center emotion of business ownership. And true business success takes more than one type of discipline. One must have the discipline to save money to start a business and the discipline to put in the long hours necessary for preparation and operation of the business. But the greatest amount of discipline has to be exercised when a business starts to succeed. The temptation to spend one's profits as a reward for one's hard efforts can be virtually overbearing. The emotional and rational aspects of your personality seem to come together and tell you that you have finally arrived. It is a temptation that has put many persons out of business needlessly.

Therefore, the other side of seeing the prosperity of Black business is not only doing the right thing to *make* a profit, but doing the right thing *with* the profits. In the early stages of a business, the almost certain thing to do is to reinvest those profits back into the business. Naturally, the business owner should have an overall strategy which might include more inventory, additional staff, a better location or additional locations.

It has been stated many times that Black people act more on emotion than reason. In business particularly, reason must win out over emotion. The respect that Black people are seeking to gain in the world of business will be determined not just by our ability to earn a profit, but by exercising sound business judgment in situations that test our will. Not only will reinvesting profits help our businesses directly, but it will also assist us in winning the support of investors and bankers. All the successful business practices in the world will come to no great end if we as businesspeople do not use our profits to stabilize our enterprise.

Commitment to Self-Education

The action-oriented people in our society attend the same schools that the rest of us do. In these schools, at both the high school and college levels, we are given an assortment of books and assignments which do very little to get us excited about the fields which interest us. The entire learning process takes place on a campus, usually divorced from anything resembling the real world. Over the course of the seven years of exposure to "educators" (three high school, four college), we actually learn to despise the very process that is to enlighten us. Boring teachers recite old notes in a monotone that would put anyone to sleep. The required courses are never explained in such a way that they tie in to our major area of interest, so they stand out in our minds as separate and unnecessary courses that relate to nothing that we can determine. The educators are too often people who have been as isolated on the campus (and apart from the real world) as the students they teach. Finally, the textbooks assigned for class are usually void of examples of practical application.

As a result of all this, action-oriented people lose virtually all regard for anything labeled "education." They have lost respect for degrees, colleges, textbooks (or books in general) and instructors. Consequently, these types of persons learn to swear by experience only, and they read virtually nothing. They don't consider themselves as losing anything, because in their minds there is nothing important, practical or relevant in books anyway, at least not in their field. Even today, one will find that many of the most action, results- and goal-oriented successful business people tend to be college drop-outs. Even though I understand very well how and why this happens, I think it is very important to coax the results-oriented person back to using some of the tools of education. There is very good and very practical information to be found in certain kinds of books. They are not the type of books that one finds in colleges. Yes, there are classes and instructors that can and will teach practical information, but they too are not to be found for the most part in your normal college classroom. One of the keys to business success is to learn how to do your enterprise better, learn what your competition is doing (or getting ready to do) and to just keep up with the general developments in your industry. Trade associations usually provide publications, classes and consultants to assist their membership. Do not be so turned off from formal instruction that you pass these learning opportunities by. As you may have heard many times by now, the United States is leaving the industrial "smokestack" industries and all indications point to the rise of informational service industries. Certainly, one cannot expect to be a businessperson fitting into the future if you as an owner turn your back on information. The reason that this point is central to get across is because self-education is a strictly optional activity. No one is going to be standing over you with a whip to make you read, attend, listen or learn. But self-education will be the key to the survival of most business people. Trial and error is a sure way to learn many things, but the lessons can be very expensive. The expense can be either in terms of lost time or it can be in actual money lost in an approach that fails to bear fruit. I have found in my personal experience that Black business people just starting out are very eager to review information which appears to be of the type that would help them in their business. I have also found, however, that those who have been in their business five years or more show a great reluctance to touch any reading material. If I could read their mind, they appear to be saying, "Unless this writer is in my business, is my color, operates in my city and deals with the same people I have to deal with, there is absolutely nothing that they can tell me. I'm not the least bit interested in reading, even if it is given to me free."

This is a sad state of events for several reasons. It not only cuts that person off from the flow of new information, but it actually discourages people, Black and White, from trying to develop materials for Black business people to keep us up to date with what is going on. But the greatest tragedy of this situation is that the non-reader is robbed of the most precious thing they have: their own ideas. You see, Black people have had such a passive attitude toward education for so long that they seem to have forgotten (if they ever knew) that the most important aspect of reading is often its function to jar loose or help you formulate *your own ideas*. In college, one memorizes for the purpose of passing tests. Out of college, one reads to find the one *missing idea* which, when connected or adopted to fit *your idea*, produces a truly *original idea*. People will inevitably learn their own way and in their own time. We are merely hoping that the printed word, whether in books or magazines, is not completely overlooked.

Crystallizing Your Ideas of Success

Much of the background information you need to get started in developing a successful business has been presented in this book. But as was stated in the section above, the greatest value of this book, as in any book, may not be what *it* specifically says so much as how it gets *you* to think. The real clarity you need to proceed more effectively with your business mission will not occur until you take out a pen, paper, and probably a calculator and actually write down where you are, where you hope to go, how you plan to get there and how long its going to take.

Primary in that task of self-examination is the process of defining your own definition of success. The word "success" is thrown at us so much that we sort of take in all the definitions and references people use and adapt them as our own. Who are you trying to please? Your family, your community, yourself, everybody? To accept everyone's definition of success as your own is to put yourself immediately *out of control.* If you currently are not accepting someone else's idea of who your spouse should be, or how many children you should have, or what would be the best religion for you, then why accept their definition of success? I have personally found vastly different definitions of success by people who were absolutely satisfied with their choice. Let me share some of them with you:

A. Experienced-Based: Because the world has so many types of people, food, music, religion, climates, countries, etc., some people have defined success in terms of their ability to taste, touch and experience as many types of experiences as the world has to offer. Money is simply the means to purchase the opportunity for these experiences. When they near death, they expect to be satisfied, feeling they've "done it all."

B. Production-Based: Many people, especially scientists and some artists, feel that their life's success should be measured by either the quality or the quantity of whatever their field dictates that they produce. Songs, books, movies, paintings, inventions, medicines, oil wells or skyscrapers are like an official point system. Each product equals a number of points, and so many points means that you won the game of life. When these people near death, they feel satisfied knowing that they "did (produce) what they were put here to do."

C. Money-Material Based: Many people measure success, as you well know, in money or material possessions. Life is full of riches, and they feel that a successful person gets their share and an unsuccessful one leaves life with their nose still pressed up against the showroom window looking in and wishing. Sometimes the money-based people only wish for the basic things associated with stardom. They would include the mansion, the beach house, the limousine, the furs and jewelry, the bank account, etc. Their definition is closely tied to the media and the latest fads. Other money people want to make more than their peers. Their definition is "outdoing" their contemporaries, whether he or she actually spends the money or not. Money, as they say, "is a means of keeping score." The last money personality I have encountered is the one with no limits. They simply want to make (and save) and accumulate as much as possible. They are usually driven by a higher form of dissatisfaction with themselves, which may or may not have a basis in a form of mental illness. I think they most probably die unsatisfied anyway.

D. Power-Based: Washington, D.C. is a great place to find the personality that sees success as defined by the position one attains that most clearly directs the fate of the masses. Of course, corporations nurture this type of personality also. The motivation for power can be to fight evil and protect the masses or it can be the result of a competitive game that simply says "the highest one on the ladder wins." In days of old, the exalted politician was always the powerful one. In times of war, the commanders of huge forces and killing power were the role models of power. Today, the leaders of the news media are called Power Kingpins because of their "power" in determining what and how the masses of the people think. In any event, money is clearly a tool to be used to muster more power (look at the huge sums poured into political campaigns). When these people near death, they wonder "how history will look at them."

Your Definition: Your definition has to make sense to you. You must draw on others because we all live in the world at large and also because others' perception of us is occasionally more accurate of us than our own. We must study our assets and the resources we have available to us. We must develop challenges but yet be "realistic." Your definition hopefully must be open for periodic examination and adjustment. As you progress, you are likely to do so faster or more slowly than you had planned, so your goals should adjust accordingly. The best piece of advice I can leave you with is to try to define your goal in such a way that the *process of getting there* is as much fun as actually arriving there. If you can really get yourself in that position, in my book you are already a very successful person.

GOOD LUCK!

INFORMATIONAL RESOURCES

Every once in a while I will hear a brother or sister say, "The reason Blacks don't have any money is because the Whites don't want us to know how to make money; they keep all the information to themselves." This is both a common and a strong belief in our community and if one were to examine our school system, the statement would seem quite valid. That is why it is important for individuals to understand that it is their *personal responsibility* to find the information themselves on the almighty dollar. Fortunately, the task is easy *because* White folks have not only exposed some of the information, they have flooded the market with just about everything you can think of. If books aren't enough, the yellow pages are full of the names of business consultants who will come to your door and spoonfeed you whatever you need if you are willing to pay the price.

This section is set up to provide information on both general market information references and Black references to information. I have found that the competent Black businessperson must stay on top of both information sources to keep up with their area of business and their market.

I should also say that the fact that a publication or organization is mentioned here does not necessarily mean that we subscribe completely to their philosophy or approach. It means solely that we have reason to believe that people in the past have gotten some benefit out of the source and there is reason to believe that this will continue.

On the other hand, because a book, or group was not included, it doesn't mean that they were discounted. It simply means that in our estimation business was not their priority or they were just unknown to us. If one is seeking the most complete directory of information on Black people, by far our best recommendation is *The Blackbook International Reference Guide* (see below).

Black Organizations

The following organizations are listed in an effort to put readers in contact with groups most consistently engaged in Black business development.

Black Association of Minority Automobile Dealers
11000 West McNichols
Detroit, Michigan 48221
(313) 863-3655

    Advocates the growth of minority car dealerships and assists those dealerships once they come into being.

National Student Business League
4324 Georgia Ave., N.W.
Washington, D.C. 20011
(202) 829-5900

    An arm of the National Business League, this organization is based primarily on Black College campuses and has a membership of students interested or majoring in various aspects of business.

National Center for Neighborhood Enterprise
1367 Connecticut Ave., N.W.
Washington, D.C.
(202) 331-1103

    A research demonstration and development organization that assists communities in using their own resources for housing, business development and self-sufficiency.

Financial Independence Institute
407 S. Dearborn, Suite 1150
Chicago, IL 60605
(312) 922-3194
    Assists Blacks in financial planning strategies, investment strategies and other financial matters.

National Bankers Association
122 C St., N.W., Suite 240
Washington, D.C. 20001
(202) 783-3200

National headquarters for the organization that encompasses all the nations' Black Banks. Runs educational programs and publishes materials for its members. Reference point on locating a local Black bank.

American Health and Beauty Aids Institute
111 East Wacker Dr., Suite 600
Chicago, IL 60601
(312) 644-6610

A trade association for Black-owned beauty and health product manufacturers. Helps promote the success of its members and contributes to business and economic development of minority communities.

American Association of Black Women Entrepreneurs, Inc.
1326 Missouri Avenue, N.W., Suite 4
Washington, D.C. 20011
(202) 231-3751

A new organization, it plans chapters in other cities for the purpose of helping Black women business owners through educational and support programs.

American Association of Minority Enterprise
Small Business Investment Companies
915 15th St., N.W., Suite 700
Washington, D.C. 20005
(202) 347-8600

The national headquarters for investment companies who are licensed by the Small Business Administration to provide capital to businesses owned by "socially and economically disadvantaged Americans."

Push International Trade Bureau
930 East 50th St.
Chicago, IL 60615
(312) 373-3366

An arm of Operation Push, this entity seeks to organize Black businesses in order to obtain a more equitable distribution of profits from corporate America. Its agreements with major American corporations on the issue of Black franchises is well known.

American League of Financial Institutions
1435 G Street, N.W., Suite 1001
Washington, D.C. 20005
(202) 628-5624

Headquarters for the organization of Black owned Savings and Loan Associations. These Savings and Loans promote home ownership by minority groups.

National Association of Market Developers
201 Ashby Street, N.W., Suite 306
Atlanta, GA 30314
(404) 688-9075

This group is made up of Black corporate employees who assist their company in relating to and selling to the Black community. An excellent place to contact key people within the Fortune 500 for minority purchasing.

Opportunity Funding Corporation
2021 K Street, N.W., Suite 701
Washington, D.C. 20006
(202) 833-9580

A non-profit organization which has as its purpose to develop and test ways of channeling private investments into poor communities and minority enterprises.

National Association of Black Women Entrepreneurs
P.O. Box 1375
Detroit, Michigan 48231
(313) 961-7714

The purpose of the NABWE, which is supported by annual national conferences, regional seminars and the "Making Success Happen" Newsletter is to assist the development, management, exposure and profitability of the Black Women Entrepreneur. The focus is on the financial, political, managerial, technical, mechanical and motivational aspects of the start up, growth and expansion of a business or venture.

National Business League
4324 Georgia Avenue, N.W.
Washington, D.C. 20011

America's oldest Black national business organization was founded in 1900 by Booker T. Washington. It speaks as the voice of the minority private sector and represents 20,000 members and 120 chapters in 37 states and the District of Columbia.

National Minority Business Council, Inc.
235 East 42nd St.
New York, NY 10017

A procurement, advocacy, educational and training organization servicing minority vendors. NMBC's primary objective is to develop the marketing, sales and management skills of its members in hopes of increasing their overall profitability.

National Minority Supplier Development Council
1412 Broadway, 11th Floor
New York, NY 10018

Formerly the National Minority Purchasing Council, the basic function of this service agency is to increase purchases of goods and services from minority-owned companies by corporate members (and others) of NMSDC. This is done through a network of 52 regional councils, operating in seven districts.

Interracial Council for Business Opportunity
800 Second Avenue, Rm. 307
New York, NY 10017
(212) 599-0677

The interracial Council for Business Opportunity, founded in 1963, is a full service business development organization devoted exclusively to minority business development.

Minority Business Legal Defense and Education Fund, Inc.
318 Massachusetts Ave., N.E.
Washington, D.C. 20005
(202) 543-0040

The Fund's mission is to defend and uphold the legality of minority set-aside programs at the state, local and national levels, to ensure the vigorous enforcement of these regulations and to initiate legal action where they are clearly being violated.

The Institute of International Trade and Development
615 E Street, N.E.
Washington, D.C. 20003
(202) 544-6300

The Institute facilitates the exchange of information on U.S. laws, regulations and practices that impact on the economic development of Third World nations and disseminates to the United States pertinent information on statutory regulatory structures of said nations.

National Association of Minority Contractors
1250 Eye St., N.W., Suite 505
Washington, D.C. 20005
(202) 347-8259

Established in 1969, NAMC is a nonprofit, membership

advocacy organization representing black, Puerto Rican, Mexican-American, native American and Asian-American contractors from 30 states, the District of Columbia and the Virgin Islands.

National Association of Real Estate Brokers
1101 14th St., N.W., Suite 900
Washington, D.C. 20005
(202) 289-6655

The oldest and largest minority trade association serving the nation's housing industry by working towards entrepreneurial development for minorities and the promotion of fair housing.

National Society of Certified Public Accountants
12700 South Bishop
Chicago, IL 60643
(312) 385-8198

Encourages blacks in business professions to seek careers in public accounting and become certified public accountants. The organization also strives to be of greater benefit to the business community, especially black businesses.

National Association of Milliners, Dressmakers and
        Tailors, Inc.
157 W. 126th St.
New York, N.Y. 10027
(212) 666-1320

Conducts networking seminars and workshops on a bi-annual basis for the exchange of skills experiences and ideas between persons working in major textile and apparel companies, in the theater and as free-lance designers and stylists.

National Beauty Culturists League
25 Logan Circle, N.W.
Washington, D.C. 20005
(202) 332-2695

Operating through 26 state chapters and two in Nassau, Bahamas, the league promotes continued education in the field of cosmetology.

National Black MBA Association
111 E. Wacker Drive, Suite 600
Chicago, IL 80801
(312) 644-6610

A nonprofit organization of minority MBA's in both the private and public sectors nationwide, membership is comprised primarily of MBA graduates and those students pursuing the advanced degree. Currently 70 percent of the approximately 1,500 members in 14 chapters across the United States are graduates from the top ten business schools in the nation.

National Association of Negro Business and Professional
    Women's Clubs, Inc.
1806 New Hampshire Avenue, N.W.
Washington, D.C. 20009
(202) 483-4206

NANBPWC has worked to create and develop opportunities and encourage training and entrance into the business and professional worlds for women, and to foster united action for improved social and civic conditions through its clubs in over 200 cities located in the United States and Africa.

National Economic Association
c/o Dean, School of Business
Kentucky State University
Frankfort, Kentucky 40601
(502) 564-5708

Founded as the Caucus of Black Economists in 1969, the organization is comprised of black economists dedicated to promoting their professional life, to advancing the study and understanding of economic problems confronting the black community and to increasing the number of black economists.

Black Authors on the Black Economic Experience

I regret to say that there is still very little information produced by Black people about their economic condition. There is even less to choose from in the way of *how-to* material written from a Black perspective. This is not to say that there has not been a recent increase of business books by Blacks; however, in view of our informational needs, we are very far behind. I am constantly asked why I think this situation exists. Because future writers of materials may be reading this particular book, I'd like to offer my opinions.

Most Black writers fall into two categories, artists and academicians. The artists write materials which are the result of personal experiences or feelings and are most often presented in autobiographical or fictional forms. Poetry is also very popular. Most Black writers probably fit into the artist-as-story-teller category. It is also very well known that it is from these types of works that movies and television scripts and plays are developed. Book sales of fictional material almost always outsell "serious" or nonfictional materials. Thus one's personal experiences, Black tradition and economic incentives all support writing fictional material. *Economic studies are not fictional.*

The other area of Black writing is in the area of academic work. Many Black educators who decide to get doctorate degrees have to write a PhD dissertation. In order for a dissertation to be accepted, a group of college professors (who form the dissertation committee) must be impressed with the *academic quality* of the work produced by the Black educator. A Master's Thesis is also judged in a similar way. Therefore, the very nature of the work produced by our Black thinker is written to please the White academic community and not the common Black person in the work-day world. If the Black PhD candidate wins the degree and moves into teaching, the next big hurdle is to win tenure at the college where they are teaching. In order to win tenure, a professor must impress their tenure committee which is usually composed of the senior professors of the department (usually they are white and advanced in age). The same type of writing that the individual produced to earn a PhD is now needed to merely have a stable job (win tenure). With a doctorate degree in hand and tenure assured, the Black academic now might seek to produce a book. Having been programmed with years of vocabulary, writing style and interests reflecting his or her academic training and environment, they usually produce the so-called "scholarly work" that few people can relate to and which is sold at virtually no retail bookstores. The idea of writing to interest the common man (or even not so common) rarely enters the head of the Black professor type. All of these reasons contribute to the lack of adequate financial information to the general Black population.

Nevertheless, a few publications are on the market and should be of interest to many Black readers.

Black Folks Guide to Making Big Money In America, by George Trower-Subira. Published by Very Serious Business Enterprise, P.O. Box 356, Newark, NJ 07101.

The first practical guidebook for Blacks on personal money management and income improvement. It discusses the common characteristics of wealthy people and the role of creativity in business operations. It assists the reader in outlining a personal plan of wealth accumulation.

The Black Woman's Career Guide, by Beatrice Nivens. Anchor Press, Doubleday Book Co., New York, NY.

Ms. Nivens is a feature writer for *Esssence* magazine and constantly travels around the country giving lectures to Black women on career choices and options. Although this volume is much more oriented toward job occupations than private business, it does offer guidance and a Black perspective to those who need it.

Black Life in Corporate America, by George Davis and Glegg Watson. Anchor Press, Doubleday Book Co., New York, NY.

The authors of this work interviewed many Black corporate employees in an effort to obtain their perspective of this American powerbase. The results are pretty much what any reader would expect. Blacks felt isolated from the real power sources in the company and limited in their career or financial goals. Many Blacks made a special effort to disclaim their Blackness in an effort to gain corporate approval. A significant number of Blacks complained about the response of Black supervisors and executives in their relationships with junior Black employees. It is beneficial to have documentation for our gut level suspicions and this is the basic contribution of this book.

The Black Manager—Making It In the Corporate World, Floyd and Jacqueline Dickens. AMACOM, American Management Association, New York, NY.

This work is published by a company which specializes in selling training material to all of Corporate America. The book assumes a very analytical-technical posture in giving suggestions to the Black corporate employee. Very helpful for those who are interested and committed to staying in the corporate world.

Racism and Sexism in Corporate Life, by Dr. John P. Fernandez. Lexington Books, D.C. Heath and Co., 125 Spring St., Lexington, Mass. 02173.

Dr. Fernandez is a brother who started a study initially designed to determine if minorities and women needed special training to become effective managers in corporations. What was discovered was that corporate management, formerly 95% white male, was experiencing turmoil throughout because of the new value systems brought in by young people, females, Blacks, Hispanics, Asians and other new manager types. This book is good because it allows the reader to view the broad spectrum of minority experiences rather than just the Black experience in isolation.

All About Success for the Black Woman, by Naomi Sims, Doubleday Books, Garden City, NY

Naomi Sims was a very successful model for years who eventually started her own company (wig business) and diversified her interests when her modeling career ended. In this book she shares her advice and philosophy regarding balancing all of life's important responsibilities. She touches on starting a business but also is speaking to the careerist in matters such as clothes, grooming, money management, etc. A good general book for women.

The Economics and Politics of Race: An International Perspective, by Thomas Sowell. William Morrow and Company, Inc., New York, NY.

Of the entire population of twenty-eight million Black Americans, I cannot think of anyone who is more misunderstood and unappreciated than Dr. Thomas Sowell. Perhaps this is because people have listened to what people have said *about him* rather than actually reading his publications.

In this particular volume, Dr. Sowell examines other minority groups in various parts of the world and analyzes their approach to economic improvement. He then directly or indirectly compares these approaches to the strategies of Black Americans. The insight one gains about our people after these comparisons is truly enlightening. This book is not recommended for identifying specific business ideas.

Ethnic America, by Thomas Sowell, William Morrow and Company, New York, NY.

Ethnic America traces the rise of various groups of Americans in a way that allows one to see the foundations of their success. It is similar to the volume above in that one gets a better appreciation of our situation and challenge by seeing how others have made it. The real challenge is being able to distinguish those principles that are universal from those that were obviously based on racial solidarity.

How To Be A Rich Nigger, Hustling—The Art of Survival, Street Economics, All by Rufus Shaw, Rufus Shaw Publications, Dallas, TX.

Everything by Rufus Shaw is controversial; his looks, his speeches and his books (even their titles). Rufus Shaw serves a function that is not being undertaken by any other writer. He is talking to what has been referred to as the "permanent underclass," the hustlers, the dope dealers, the convicts and the permanently unemployed. He is talking to them about money, through poetry, slang and short statements. I have no doubt that quite a few have changed their attitudes since reading his work.

Black Business and Economics, by George H. Hill, Garland Press.

At press time, we had not seen this book. However, it appears to be a bibliography of books and articles about Black Economics.

Black Publications

Magazines

Black Enterprise, 295 Madison Avenue, New York, NY 10017 (212) 889-8220

The most relevant regular publication for Black folks seeking to improve their economic situation. Many articles on the heavy issues that face the Black businessperson and the community at large. Many success stories and an excellent source to gain contacts with the people who are doing what you want to do.

Dollars and Sense Magazine, 1610 E. 79th St., Chicago, IL 60649 (312) 375-6800

Dollars and Sense Magazine, a Black publication, can be described in one word—comprehensive! No Black publication in the U.S. goes into as much detail in its subject matter. When they cover an issue, they blanket it. Covers the Black consumer market, corporate profiles and Black professional organizations.

Financial Independence Money Management Magazine, 1519 Pennsylvania Avenue, S.E., Washington, D.C. 20003 (202) 547-3803

This new publication (1985) is addressed to the average Black reader who wishes to improve their personal finances. Concentrates on the practical day to day issues of the individual rather than focusing on research, corporate views or leisure time activities. Shows much promise for the future.

Ebony and *Jet* Magazines, 820 D Michigan Ave., Chicago, IL 60605 (312) 322-9200

Ebony frequently features articles of economic significance but they usually include more photographs than nitty-gritty information, even in features on business personalities.

Jet usually gives a page per issue to highlight the economic news and announcements of the previous week.

Shop Talk, 407 S. Dearborn, Suite 925, Chicago, IL 60605

This publication is a very slick, very professional trade journal for people in the hair care and beauty industry. It is available at newstands and would be of interest to many non-beauty businesspeople because it contains so many inspiring Black success stories. The many tips on improving salon service, customer service and general business practices would be sound advice for any black businessperson.

Essence, 1500 Broadway, New York, NY 10036 (212) 730-4260

In the last five years, this publication has made great strides in highlighting successful black female owned businesses. Generally a women's magazine, *Essence* should be read by any man who intends to market to the female market. No black publication does a better job in reviewing the lastest books by black authors.

Black Family Magazine, 332 N. Michigan Ave., Chicago, IL 60601 (312) 855-0200

Although a family magazine covering a full line of general issues (health, cooking, child care, etc.), this publication usually interviews a business or professional role model. These interviews capture a perspective that is not typical of any other publications.

Élancée, P.O. Box 60680-8257, Chicago, IL 60680 (312) 939-7000

Another women's magazine similar to *Essence* in style. Definitely aimed at the business and professional woman and thus has articles on nontraditional topics like sales or women in executive positions.

Focus Magazine, 475 Fifth Avenue, Suite 608, New York, NY 10017

A publication which appears to take on serious black issues even on an international basis. Each issue contains significant material on the status of blacks in a profession or on an aspect of black (or personal) economics.

Washington Living Magazine, 6506 McCahill Dr., Laurel, MD 20707 (301) 495-2801

A general family magazine covering black life in and around the capital. Consistently produces at least two articles per issue with economic relevance.

Black Collegian, 1240 S. Broad St., New Orleans, LA 70125 (504) 821-5694

A very mature, well supported, slick magazine for black college students. Very comprehensive on a variety of issues and good interviews.

No black publication includes more information on career development. Unfortunately, this magazine reflects the exact problem of colleges. Namely, they always assume black graduates will be working for somebody else. I have never seen an article on entrepreneurship in this publication.

Taking Care of Business, Seagram's Guide to Taking Care of Business, 375 Park Ave., New York, N.Y. 10152
This is a magazine coming out periodically which is produced by a sister and her company, G. Joyce Hamer of Hamer Advertising and Marketing Concepts (Homeconcepts, Inc.). This publication appears to be totally underwritten by Seagram's Distillers. It features articles similar to *Black Enterprise* in terms of its mixture: corporate, entrepreneurial, personal finance and living the good live (travel, food, etc.). I have never seen a dull issue. Not available at newstands but is given away free at liquor stores.

Newsletters

The Puryear Money Report, P.O. Box 2582, Brooklyn, N.Y 11202. (212) 889-0122.
Milton Puryear and spouse Yla Eason Puryear have developed quite a record in tracking stocks and bonds and other investment vehicles. Don't bother to check it out unless you are very serious. Milton is clear but very analytical (I guess that's why he's good).

Black Money—based in Washington, D.C. area—no address available at press time.
Another newsletter directed to minorities about investing in the stock market.

Minority Business Review, P.O. Box 2132, Hempstead, N.Y. 11550 (516) 489-0120
A newsletter-newspaper dedicated to information about minority business. Keeps its readers informed on bids for state contracts. Centered principally on New York City and N.Y. state but carries some national news summaries.

Directories — Black Organizations and Institutions

Blackbook International Reference Guide, National Publication Sales Agency, Inc., 1610 E. 79th St., Chicago, IL 60649 (312) 374-6800

The same company that produces *Dollars and Sense Magazine* (the comprehensive monthly) produces this directory. I cannot honestly say that it is possible to produce a more complete document on how to contact important black people, organizations and networks. I personally have used this document at least once every two weeks or so for the last two years.

The Black Resource Guide, 501 Oneida Place, N.W., Washington, D.C. 20011

A very, very good compilation of information on locating major black organizations and businesses.

Major Black Business Events

Bronner Brothers Beauty Show, 903 Martin Luther King Jr. Drive, Atlanta, GA 30310 (404) 577-4321

Mainly a hair care show but a little of everything is represented. Plan to book your space up to a year in advance. Its gets bigger every year.

Black Expo Showcase, 2403 E. 75th St., Chicago, IL 60649 (312) 374-4380

The largest business expo that I am aware of. Takes place in Chicago and Atlanta in the Fall of each year.

Blackbook National Business and Professional Awards Banquet, 1610 E. 79th St., Chicago, IL 60649 (312) 375-6800

Annual dinner honoring the heavy hitters in black business. Usually takes place mid to late February every year.

Indiana Black Expo, Indianapolis, Indiana (317) 925-2702

Business and community people hold workshops and display wares at the largest gathering of black folk in the city for the year. Usually happens late July.

Mainstream Business Magazines

The amount of information that White America produces on making the dollar is incredible. I am convinced that I will never come close to finding them all and you probably won't either. The important thing I feel is that a person finds the right mix of information to feed their minds or spirits whenever either one needs a shot of juice. We all have "down" moments and I personally beat mine off with new information. Try it; you'll like it.

Money Magazine, Time-Life Corp., New York, N.Y. $1.75 per issue at news-stand.

One of the two most important regular publications for the Black person looking to make money. This magazine is a constantly running faucet of information of who is doing what to build fortunes. Success stories, specials on tax, real estate, bargain hunting, stock and other developments are regular features. At the end of the periodical are many ads where the aspiring businessperson can look over the newest franchise type operations that are available.

The American Salesman, published by the National Research Bureau, 104 S. Michigan Avenue, Chicago, Illinois (312) 641-2655.

A how to sell magazine which gives salespersons a constantly running stream of ideas. One recent article was called "Using Your Eyes In Selling." Now that's getting down if you can get to it.

Changing Times (Kiplinger-Washington editors). $1.25 per issue, Editors Park, Maryland 20781.

A family type of magazine dedicated to stretching the budget dollar. Special Reports on things like fuel saving ideas, food shopping hints, real estate trends, tax tips and all other basic cost cutting measures.

Salesman's Opportunity, 6N Michigan Avenue, Chicago, Illinois. $1.25 per issue.

A what's-going-on-in-the-world-of-the-direct-salesperson's-life type of publication. A top source for finding out what the hottest gimmicks are (before it's too late to cash in on them) and what profits can be generated. Also addresses the common problems of salespersons and includes many motivational articles.

Inc., 38 Commercial Wharf, Boston, Mass. 02110. (617) 227-4700.
The magazine for the owner-officer of the small but substantial company of a half million dollars or more. Deals with the problems of growth and the many gray areas that million dollar corporations find themselves in.

The Big Company Magazines: *Business Week, Forbes, Fortune, Financial World.*
These magazines address themselves to the presidents and top officers of large corporations on the international issues (oil embargo, the European common market, world gold supply, etc.) of the day. Although you could pick up some interesting ideas by reading these magazines, the greater possibility is that the information is too broad to be of any use to you in your immediate goals.

Venture, 35 W. 45th St., New York, NY 10036 (212) 840-5580.
Bills itself as the magazine for entrepreneurs and that's exactly what it is. Most of the companies they describe are in the million dollar per year gross sales category. This is very good in the sense that it gives you an idea of what kinds of things to prepare for down the road but it doesn't help much in the crucial crank-up stage of development. The publication covers all areas of interest to the new businessperson: tax laws, franchises, insurance, computer applications and, of course, good interviews of success models. *Venture* is especially good at interviewing corporate employees who have made the move to starting their own thing.

In Business, Box 323, 18 S. 7th St., Emmaus, PA 18049. (215) 967-4135.
In Business is of particular interest to people just starting out in their enterprise. Like *Venture*, it covers all the bases, like marketing, direct mail, management, legal issues, etc., but from the point of view of a smaller company. In the dozen or so articles they usually cover things like couples working together or working at home, starting up, financing ideas, etc. A good publication, but not as widely distributed as most others.

Entrepreneur, 2311 Pontius Avenue, Los Angeles, CA 90064. (213) 477-1011.

In my opinion, this publication is the single best publication for late-breaking business ideas. They go deep in the woods to find people who have been successful in the newest fad you can think of. The problem is that while they encourage and inspire any warm body to get going, they appear to give the impression that it is much easier than it is. The parent company sells a tremendous amount of business start-up information which may seem very expensive until you realize that consultants or your time in research would cost more. You have got to get a new idea after reading a few of these issues; it's almost impossible not to.

Success Magazine, 342 Madison avenue, New York, NY 10173 (212) 503-0700.

This publication is a little different from the others in that it often probes very important but rarely discussed psychological aspects of business success. How do successful people think, stay motivated or cope with hassles? How do employers treat employees or executives relate to higher corporate decision makers? These issues are prominent in a publication which also has its share of success stories, late breaking news, book reviews and investment information. A very good publication.

Home Office, Time, Inc., Rockefeller Center, New York, NY 10020.

The same people who put together *Money Magazine* now have a new publication especially designed for people who operate a business out of their home. This is a new publication (1985) and combines many aspects found in dissimilar publications into one. For example, interior decorating has nothing to do with business or computers until they become the interests of a self-employed at home business person. This publication hits the common concerns of temporary help, in home tax writeoffs, phone systems and even staying fit in the home office. A very, very good publication.

Working Woman, 1180 Avenue of the Americas, New York, NY 10036. (212) 944-5250.

Is designed for today's "superwoman" who tries to balance career, family and personal life into one working whole and still sleep. Articles include looking at the corporate world from the feminine point of view, trends in graduate education, personal money management, entrepreneurship, as well as the regular "woman's areas" of fashion, children, food and health. A good complement to *Essence Magazine*.

Savvy, 111 Eighth Avenue, Suite 1517, New York, NY 10011. (212) 255-0990.

Savvy is a lot like *Working Woman* except they seem to interview more successful women business owners and higher level corporate executives. I refer to *Savvy* as the *Black Enterprise* for women and sometimes I get as much out of it as I do the latter.

Income Opportunities, 380 Lexington Ave., New York, NY 10017. (212) 557-9100.

This publication is full of ads by companies interested in offering business propositions. The opportunities run the whole line between flimsy to very interesting so one must do their homework before investing. This magazine often analyzes or describes the opportunity of their advertisers and explains things that one cannot get from a normal display ad. This is something few other publications do. Also, they do book condensations of how-to-books so you have a good idea of what a new publication contains before shelling out your money.

Progressive Bookstores
(or where you can buy this book)

The following people and establishments have been very key over the years in providing a place where people can consistently obtain copies of the publications of Very Serious Business Enterprises. Should you live in or near these cities, you should be able to obtain additional copies of this volume right away. If you do not live near these cities, you may simply send $12.95 money order to Very Serious Business Enterprises, P.O. Box 356, Newark, NJ 07101 for each additional copy that you would like.

If you know of stores that have consistently carried our book but which are not listed in this section, please write us to let us know.

If you know of a store that you recommend we contact to carry our books please let us know about those also.

BIRMINGHAM, ALABAMA
   Know Thyself Bookstore, 808 6th St. North

PINE BLUFF, ARKANSAS
   Ebony Bookstore & Gifts, 109 E. 4th St.

SAN FRANCISCO, CALIFORNIA
   Marcus Bookstore, 1712 Filmore
   New Day Bookstore, 631 Divisadero

LOS ANGELES, CALIFORNIA
   Aquarian Bookshop, 1342 W. Martin Luther King Blvd.

DENVER, COLORADO
   Hue Man Experience, 911 23rd St.

HARTFORD, CONNECTICUT
   Huntington's Bookstore, 65 Asylum St.

WILMINGTON, DELAWARE
   Hanseef's Bookstore, 300 Market St.

WASHINGTON, D.C.
   Pyramid Bookstore, 2849 Georgia Ave. N.W.
   Benjamin Books, Washington National Airport
   Common Concerns, Inc., 1347 Connecticut Ave. N.W.
   John Raye & Associates, 1425 K St. N.W., 289-0034
   Capital Planning Corp., 1519 Pennsylvania Ave. S.E.

FLORIDA
   Ms. Liz Page (904) 893-5284, Tallahassee
   DuBey's Bookstore, Downtown & Northwood, Tallahassee
   Afro-in Books & Things, 5575 N.W. 7th Ave., Miami

ATLANTA, GEORGIA
   Reese Realtors, 37 Lynhurst
   Shrine of Black Madonna, 946 Gordon St. S.W.
   Hakims Bookstore, Martin Luther King Drive
   Alkebulon News Distributors, 1371 Gordon St. S.W.

CHICAGO, ILLINOIS
   Christ Universal Temple, Ashland Ave.
   Kroch's and Brentano's, 29 Wabash Ave.
   Mass, Inc. James Cage (312) 638-5294
   Afro-Caribbean Bookstore, 2319 E. 71st

GARY, INDIANA
   The Jesus Shop, 2210 W. 10th Ave.

LOUISVILLE, KENTUCKY
   Mr. Melvin Turner, University of Louisville (502) 423-7083
   Black Market Bookstore, P.O. Box 11115
   Hawley-Cook Booksellers, 27 Shelbyville Rd. Plaza

BATON ROUGE, LOUISIANA
Collegiate Book Store, 616 Harding Blvd.

BOSTON, MASSACHUSETTS
Barnes & Noble Downtown
Mr. Charles Penderhughes-Afro-American Booksource

DETROIT, MICHIGAN
Shrine of Black Madonna, 13535 Livernois
Doubleday Bookshop, Penobscot Building
The Book End, 6 Northland Mall-Southfield
Vaugh's Bookstore, 13140 W. 7 Mile Rd.
Arknartoon's Health Store, 10300 Woodward
Paperbacks Unlimited, 22634 Woodward, Ferndale
Afro-American Museum 1553 W. Grand Blvd.

ST. LOUIS, MISSOURI
Progressive Emporium, 6265 Delmar Blvd.
Follett Store, Busch Center, 20 North Grand
Left Bank Books, 399 N. Euclid

NEW JERSEY
New Jersey Books, Market St. & University Ave., Newark
Health Foods Store, Broad St., Newark
Bridges Bookstore, 1480 Main St., Rahway
Jade Marketing, P.O. Box 2783, Paterson 07509
The Black Book Club, Box 40, Fanwood 07023
The Book House, 218 E. Front St., Plainfield
The Post Bookstore, 597 Central, East Orange
Gordon's Alley, Atlantic City

OHIO
Shaker Square Bookshop, 13214 Shaker Sq.
Taiyyib Islamic Books, 3752 Lee Rd., Shaker Hts.
The News Depot, 207 Market Ave., Canton
Barnes & Noble, 2400 Euclid Ave., Cleveland
Wit and Wisdom, 24031 Chagrin Blvd., Beachwood
Showcase Books, 145 W. Market, Warren
Wilkie News, Inc., 123 S. Ludlow, Dayton
Kum Ba Ya Christian Bookstore, 1507 Livingston, Columbus
E.A.L. Enterprises, 22700 Shore Center Ave., Cleveland
New World Bookshop, 336 Ludlow, Cincinnati
Shillito's Distribution Center, 5121 Fishwick Dr., Cincinnati

NEW YORK CITY
Empire Baptist Bookstore, 63 W. 125th St.
Barnes & Noble Bookstore, 5th Ave. & 18th St.
Barnes & Noble Bookstore, Downtown, Brooklyn
Tents of Kedar, 549 Flatbush Ave., Brooklyn
Benjamin Books, Inc., World Trade Center

Benjamin Books, Inc., Port Authority Bldg.
Liberation Bookstore, Lenox Ave. & 131st St.
House of a Million Earrings, 153-32 Hillside Ave., Jamaica
Universal Bookstore, 51 Court, White Plains, NY
AS-SUQ, 96 Smith St., Brooklyn
United Church, 4140 Broadway (at 176th)
Radiance, 317 W. 125th, Harlem

BUFFALO, NEW YORK
Harambee Books & Crafts, 31 St. Paul Mall

ROCHESTER, NEW YORK
Amefika Gueka (716) 454-6674

PHILADELPHIA, PENNSYLVANIA
Robins Bookstore, 108 S. 13th
Hakims Bookstore, 210 S. 52nd St.
Brad Allen Bookstore, Cheltenham Square Mall
Maplewood Books, 45 Maplewood Mall
Kaumba Health Food, 2010 E. Chelten Ave.

HARRISBURG, PENNSYLVANIA
African Image Books, 501 Winaind Dr.

TENNESSEE
Yusef Harris, (615) 297-8934, Nashville
Ma Cardo Gift Shop, 164 Union, Memphis
Miles College Alumni-Earnest Jones, (901) 785-3290, Memphis
Mills Bookstore, 1817 21st Ave. South, Nashville

TEXAS
Black Images Book Bazaar, 2929 S. Westmoreland #61, Dallas (214) 375-1733
The Shoe Fair, 6316 Meadowbrook Dr., Fort Worth
Amistad Book Place, 5613 Almeda Suite 100, Houston
Shrine of Black Madonna, 5317 Martin Luther King Blvd., Houston
The Brown Book Shop, 1219 Fannin, Houston

NORTH CAROLINA
Bruce Lightner, 755-0804, Raleigh
McLaughlins Pharmacy, 2520 Fayetteville, Durham
Undercover Bookstore, 115 East Blvd., Charlotte

SOUTH CAROLINA
Mann-Simons Cottage, 1403 Richland, Columbia

VIRGINIA
Cokesbury Bookstore, 417 E. Grace St., Richmond
The Bookery, Rt. #13 Shoppers Village, Tasley
House of Umaja, 2015 Jefferson Ave., Newport News

MILWAUKEE, WISCONSIN
Integrity Books, 116 W. Wright St.

WEST VIRGINIA
Smith's Arcade News, 710 Virginia St., East Charleston
Major's Book Store, 221 Hale St., Charleston

Very Serious Business Enterprises
Distributor Opportunity

Very Serious Business Enterprises is a company with two primary
goals:

1. To develop, distribute and sell books and materials specifically
    designed to educate Black Americans about business and/or
    economic advancement.

2. To distribute and sell materials (books, audio tapes, video tapes,
    etc.) developed by others which we feel will help Black Americans
    in their personal, professional, business or economic development.

In carrying out our purpose and goals we have gained at least three
tangible rewards:

*   We have seen specific economic gains by many of our readers
*   We have made fair profits
*   We have built excellent contacts and networks

> We have found that the best means of getting our products to the
> people they were designed for is through a network of individual
> distributors. Our distributors, like ourselves, have gained fair profits,
> interesting and supportive contacts and the satisfaction of helping peo-
> ple improve their financial circumstances.

Any person, business, organization or group can become a distributor
of our material. By simply purchasing a minimum number of books (ten)
a distributor is entitled to the wholesale rates. The discounts for our other
products vary according to the specific products.

We welcome anyone who desires to join us in pushing for the development of more and better businesses for Black people.

PHOTOCOPY THIS PAGE (or type the appropriate information) and fill in the requested information below. Send it to:

VERY SERIOUS BUSINESS ENTERPRISES
P.O. Box 356
Newark, N.J. 07101
(609) 641-0776

☐ Add my name to your mailing list. I'd like a chance to examine any opportunity you wish to share with your readers. I am under no obligation to buy or sell anything.

☐ I'd like to order additional copies of this book. Enclosed is a check or money order of $12.95 for each copy I am requesting.

☐ I'd like to sell your book from my shop, store, stand or business. Please send me information on how I can be a distributor.

☐ I'd like to order a large quantity of your books to sell in our fund raising efforts for our church, day care center, or other neighborhood program.

Name_____

Address_____

City_____State_____Zip_____

Telephone _____ Occupation _____

Major Business Interest _____